Communicating in College Classrooms

Jean M. Civikly, *Editor*

NEW DIRECTIONS FOR TEACHING AND LEARNING
KENNETH E. EBLE, *Editor-in-Chief*

Number 26, June 1986

Paperback sourcebooks in
The Jossey-Bass Higher Education Series

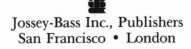

Jossey-Bass Inc., Publishers
San Francisco • London

Jean M. Civikly (Ed.).
Communicating in College Classrooms.
New Directions for Teaching and Learning, no. 26.
San Francisco: Jossey-Bass, 1986.

New Directions for Teaching and Learning
Kenneth E. Eble, *Editor-in-Chief*

New Directions for Teaching and Learning is published quarterly
by Jossey-Bass Inc., Publishers.

Correspondence:
Subscriptions, single-issue orders, change of address notices,
undelivered copies, and other correspondence should be sent to
Subscriptions, Jossey-Bass Inc., Publishers, 433 California Street,
San Francisco, California 94104.

Editorial correspondence should be sent to the Editor-in-Chief,
Kenneth E. Eble, Department of English, University of Utah,
Salt Lake City, Utah 84112.

Library of Congress Catalog Card Number 85-81904

International Standard Serial Number ISSN 0271-0633

International Standard Book Number ISBN 87589-736-3

Cover art by WILLI BAUM

Manufactured in the United States of America

Ordering Information

The paperback sourcebooks listed below are published quarterly and can be ordered either by subscription or single-copy.

Subscriptions cost $40.00 per year for institutions, agencies, and libraries. Individuals can subscribe at the special rate of $30.00 per year *if payment is by personal check.* (Note that the full rate of $40.00 applies if payment is by institutional check, even if the subscription is designated for an individual.) Standing orders are accepted.

Single copies are available at $9.95 when payment accompanies order, and *all single-copy orders under $25.00 must include payment.* (California, New Jersey, New York, and Washington, D.C., residents please include appropriate sales tax.) For billed orders, cost per copy is $9.95 plus postage and handling. (Prices subject to change without notice.)

Bulk orders (ten or more copies) of any individual sourcebook are available at the following discounted prices: 10–49 copies, $8.95 each; 50–100 copies, $7.96 each; over 100 copies, *inquire.* Sales tax and postage and handling charges apply as for single copy orders.

To ensure correct and prompt delivery, all orders must give either the *name of an individual* or an *official purchase order number.* Please submit your order as follows:

> *Subscriptions:* specify series and year subscription is to begin.
> *Single Copies:* specify sourcebook code (such as, TL1) and first two words of title.

Mail orders for United States and Possessions, Latin America, Canada, Japan, Australia, and New Zealand to:
> Jossey-Bass Inc., Publishers
> 433 California Street
> San Francisco, California 94104

Mail orders for all other parts of the world to:
> Jossey-Bass Limited
> 28 Banner Street
> London EC1Y 8QE

New Directions for Teaching and Learning Series
Kenneth E. Eble, *Editor-in-Chief*

TL1 *Improving Teaching Styles,* Kenneth E. Eble
TL2 *Learning, Cognition, and College Teaching,* Wilbert J. McKeachie
TL3 *Fostering Critical Thinking,* Robert E. Young
TL4 *Learning About Teaching,* John F. Noonan

TL5   *The Administrator's Role in Effective Teaching*, Alan E. Guskin

TL6   *Liberal Learning and Careers*, Charles S. Green, III, Richard G. Salem

TL7   *New Perspectives on Teaching and Learning*, Warren Bryan Martin

TL8   *Interdisciplinary Teaching*, Alvin M. White

TL9   *Expanding Learning Through New Communications Technologies*, Christopher K. Knapper

TL10   *Motivating Professors to Teach Effectively*, James L. Bess

TL11   *Practices that Improve Teaching Evaluation*, Grace French-Lazovik

TL12   *Teaching Writing in All Disciplines*, C. Williams Griffin

TL13   *Teaching Values and Ethics in College*, Michael J. Collins

TL14   *Learning in Groups*, Clark Bouton, Russell Y. Garth

TL15   *Revitalizing Teaching Through Faculty Development*, Paul A. Lacey

TL16   *Teaching Minority Students*, James H. Cones, III, John F. Noonan, Denise Janha

TL17   *The First Year of College Teaching*, L. Dee Fink

TL18   *Increasing the Teaching Role of Academic Libraries*, Thomas G. Kirk

TL19   *Teaching and Aging*, Chandra M. N. Mehrotra

TL20   *Rejuvenating Introductory Courses*, Karen I. Spear

TL21   *Teaching as Though Students Mattered*, Joseph Katz

TL22   *Strengthening the Teaching Assistant Faculty*, John D. W. Andrews

TL23   *Using Research to Improve Teaching*, Janet C. Donald, Arthur M. Sullivan

TL24   *College-School Collaboration: Appraising the Major Approaches*, William T. Daly

TL25   *Fostering Academic Excellence Through Honors Programs*, Paul G. Friedman, Reva Jenkins-Friedman

Contents

Editor's Notes   1
Jean M. Civikly

Chapter 1. Instructor Communication Habits: 5
Confrontation and Challenge
Jean M. Civikly
Why are faculty reluctant to work on their own communication skills?
The author explores ways to confront one's communication habits and to
meet three challenges for refining one's instructional communication.

Chapter 2. The Ethnocentric Classroom   11
John C. Condon
Mixing the academic culture of a classroom with the cultural diversity of
its students often results unintentionally in an ethnocentric classroom. The
teacher's view of what is appropriate class behavior is likely to be foreign
to some of the students.

Chapter 3. Communication Apprehension in the   21
College Classroom
John A. Daly
When students dislike and avoid communicating, learning falters and goals
are unlikely to be achieved. The development of communication apprehension, its behavioral manifestations, and strategies for overcoming it are
discussed.

Chapter 4. Communicator Style in Teaching: 33
Giving Good Form to Content
Robert W. Norton
A teacher's style of communication tells students how to interpret the
instructional content and affects students' feelings toward the teacher and
the class. Different communicator styles are identified, with special attention to the components of a dramatic style.

Chapter 5. Instructor Nonverbal Communication: 41
Listening to Our Silent Messages
Janis F. Andersen
Nonverbal messages provide information to students about the instructor's
preferences for interpersonal support, genuineness, and power. These messages also have a direct impact on the students' motivation to learn and
attitudes toward content.

Chapter 6. Teaching as Relational Development   **51**
Joseph A. DeVito

Education is a process of relational development between students and teachers and is dependent on effective interpersonal communication. Seven stages of this relational development and nine relational skills for teachers are discussed.

Chapter 7. Humor and the Enjoyment of College Teaching   **61**
Jean M. Civikly

Humor in teaching can promote a positive and cohesive class atmosphere, but it can also have unintended negative results if the teacher does not first develop a supportive relationship with the students.

Chapter 8. Teacher-Student Confrontations   **71**
Joyce L. Hocker

Although conflicts are inevitable, they need not be destructive. Characteristics of productive conflicts and conflict-management styles are discussed, with special attention to collaborative tactics and alternatives.

Chapter 9. The Art of Teaching: An Act of Love   **83**
Joel M. Jones

The author's reflections on the arts and acts of teaching and loving result in several conclusions about the higher aims of college instruction: Self transcends technique; authenticity precedes authority; and vulnerability precludes venerability.

Chapter 10. Meeting the Challenge   **93**
Jean M. Civikly

Further suggestions and resources for developing communication skills are provided.

Index   **99**

Editor's Notes

From our experiences as students and teachers, we know that messages in classrooms can hit the bull's-eye or go awry like an unguided missile. But no matter what the impact of the message is, we can be sure of one thing: The message exists. Teachers cannot teach without communicating. Just as most college instructors lack formal teacher training, few have sufficient formal preparation in communication processes as they operate in classrooms. Too often we lapse into thinking that because we communicate, we necessarily do it well. We stop questioning or reflecting on *how* we do it and stop evaluating *how well* we do it. The unquestioning ease with which we approach our communication experiences may be our biggest obstacle to effective interaction in the classroom and elsewhere.

This collection of chapters addresses prominent classroom communication issues. The chapters deal with teachers and students as they communicate and form unique relationships with each other. As each particular topic dictates, attention to student and teacher communicative behaviors varies. One of the more *student-centered* chapters is John Daly's review of communication apprehension. Daly describes the fear of communicating, its impact on a student's academic and social performance and perception, and what teachers can do to help.

The more *teacher-centered* chapters comprise the bulk of this volume. Although the concepts and skills described therein certainly can apply to students as well, these authors stress the guiding role that teachers can play in the classroom. In the opening chapter, I suggest that teaching and communicating behaviors are established habits and offer explanations for why faculty may be reluctant to attend to their own communication skills. Robert Norton and Janis Andersen have contributed chapters that stress the teacher's *presentational* behaviors. Norton advances the ongoing discussion of teaching style and emphasizes the pragmatic concerns of communicator style. Andersen reviews the effects of various nonverbal teacher behaviors and how they have influenced students' feelings about the teacher, course, and discipline. Joseph DeVito argues that teacher-student interactions can benefit from attention to research that describes the developmental process experienced in interpersonal relationships. My chapter on teacher humor considers both the affective dimensions of learning and the importance of developing a relational base with students so that humor will promote rather than inhibit classroom interactions. In an essay on teacher-student confrontations, Joyce Hocker discusses power struggles commonly observed in classes, as well as alternative conflict-management styles and tactics for approaching such difficult encounters.

1

Rather than emphasizing behaviors specific to students or teachers, two authors, John Condon and Joel Jones, have reflected on the climate of learning in terms of the culture of the classroom and one's philosophical approach to the art of teaching. Condon's essay on the ethnocentric classroom alerts us to the invisible norms operating within the domain of any teacher's class and questions the fairness of those norms for culturally diverse student groups. Joel Jones describes teaching through the metaphor of making love: the excitement, passion, arousal, and joy experienced at moments of intellectual growth. "The knowing and the knowledge which characterize loving and learning at their best must be both verbal and visceral."

Although these authors advance the ideas of their very specific areas of expertise, the conceptual foundations of their work have much in common. Three characteristics of communication are noteworthy: Communication is systemic, transactional, and complex. The characterization of communication as *systemic* has two interpretations. First, the *process* of communication is a system governed by norms and rules that are culturally determined and usually unspoken. Two rules we assume or expect to observe in classrooms and elsewhere, for example, are to listen to the person speaking and to use verbal and nonverbal messages that have common meanings for the group addressed. Second, the *communicators* involved in the interaction, in this case teachers and students, are parts of a system. Each is dependent on the other and influences the other. Just as a machine needs to have its parts in good operating order, the classroom system cannot function smoothly without input from each person in some agreed-upon form of coordination.

The identification of communication as *transactional* brings the spotlight to the participants—the teachers and students. In a transactional approach, each participant is recognized as being simultaneously a sender and a receiver of messages. In addition, each participant has his or her unique interpretation of those messages. Thus the teacher is simultaneously explaining information and filtering student feedback at the same time as the students are listening and providing nonverbal messages. And in the midst of all this, each person in the room is likely to be carrying on an internal conversation, "self-talk." For the teacher, this self-talk might be, "I know I planned to develop a concept here. . . . I forgot what example I was going to use . . . better just move on. . . . I'm running out of time." For the student, self-talk can range from, "That's happened to me—now I get it!" to "Don't forget to pick up some dog food on the way home."

This bombardment of messages and variables operating in classroom instruction makes the characteristic of communication extremely *complex*. A two-person interaction, for example, incorporates such matters as each individual's communication abilities, past successes and failures, interest level, credibility, self-esteem, physical alertness and energy, emotional state, and mood. When this interaction expands to include a larger student collective, the complexity of classroom communication can be overwhelming. Pamela Cooper's description of the communication process speaks directly to this point when she writes, "Communication is a relationship we engage in; it is not something as simple as sending and receiving messages" (1984, p. 6).

These three communication characteristics help to explain the fascination of teaching noted by Joseph Epstein in his research on master teachers: "The relationship between teacher and student can be of supreme significance. . . . Everywhere the task of teaching is the same—this lighting of sparks, this setting aflame—and everywhere it is carried on differently. This is the inherent fascination of the subject" (1981, xvii–xviii).

The qualities unique to a class, if sought out, ensure continuation of this fascination with teaching. The authors in this volume do not give cookbook solutions to communication problems in teaching; they cannot because they do not know you and each of your student groups. Welcome the lack of prescriptive remedies. Reflect on the guidelines for analysis and application that are offered. Take on a challenge: add the ingredients needed to flesh out the guidelines—you and your students. The results may approach G. E. Frost's reflection on teaching (Cooper, 1984, p. 339):

Perhaps there is no effort
which is as total
or which makes one so vulnerable
as teaching.
He who attempts it reaches beyond himself
and senses that his best is not good enough.

Jean M. Civikly
Editor

References

Cooper, P. J. *Speech Communication for the Classroom Teacher*, 2nd ed. Dubuque, Iowa: Gorsuch Scarisbrick, 1984.
Epstein, J. (Ed.). *Masters: Portraits of Great Teachers*. New York: Basic Books, 1981.

Jean M. Civikly is associate professor of Speech Communication at the University of New Mexico. In addition to her teaching and research on the interpersonal dynamics of classroom instruction, she is director of the university's Teaching Assistant Resource Center.

Communication is the means by which teachers conduct their profession. Responding to challenges to refine instructional communication skills has both personal and professional payoffs.

Instructor Communication Habits: Confrontation and Challenge

Jean M. Civikly

The professions of teaching and acting have many similarities—both have actors and actresses, scripts, stages, audiences, and critical reviews. Whether the context is the theater or the classroom, these reviews can run the gamut from magnificent to dreadful. If the reviews are dreadful, the theater show is likely to close within days, but the teaching performance will endure for the academic term. And if the reviews are magnificent, the show is likely to play for several years, but the course will most definitely end its run in accordance with the school calendar.

A college professor's "repeat performances" each school term are predictable in a number of ways, and it is easy for the "act" of teaching to become an ingrained habit. Consider the program for a typical teaching performance:

Act I	Preparation of course content and materials
Act II	In-class appearances
Act III	Grading of papers and tests
Grand Finale	Handing in and posting grades

J. M. Civikly, (Ed.). *Communicating in College Classrooms.*
New Directions for Teaching and Learning, no. 26. San Francisco: Jossey-Bass, June 1986.

Another similarity between theater and education is the element of a *live* audience. Whether the scene is a theater or a classroom, it is the performance on the stage or at the lectern that prompts the audience to applaud, to boo, to be inspired or repulsed, or to lapse into moments of sleepy head-bobbing. Although comparisons of teaching and acting hold up rather well, as noted here and by other educational commentators (Murray, 1985; Homan, 1985; Lowman, 1984; Timpson and Tobin, 1982), one of the differences between these professions involves how each focuses on training for the career. In the theater, the emphasis is on engaging the audience and keeping its attention. In the college classroom the focus has not traditionally been on the instructor's efforts at getting the message across to the audience. Rather, successful impact (often equated with student learning) has been assumed to occur if the instructor is "content-competent," that is, if he or she knows the material (the script). Much less thought has been paid to *communication competence,* the ability to speak, listen, behave, and interact in a way that is both appropriate for the setting and effective for the desired purpose (Rubin, 1983; Spitzberg and Cupach, 1984). Accordingly, "teaching is risky, especially to new faculty, because it forces them to demonstrate a competency for which they have had no training" (Bess, 1982, p. 102).

Unless a professor has held an appointment as a teaching assistant during the years of graduate study, the opportunity for instructional rehearsals is slim. Consider the acts of stepping onto the stage and into the classroom—events that have been described as nothing less than traumatic. Yet learning from those experiences is rapid and takes several forms. For example, there are some individuals who discover or confirm that they are good at it; these are the so-called natural talents, whether the task is acting or teaching. Others realize that they are awkward at their profession—that they need to get some pointers on polishing the rough edges—and they set out to do so. Finally, there are those who are awkward in their work but avoid or reject making changes or taking steps toward improvement. For this last group, the reasons can be many. While these reasons are likely to apply to acting as well as to teaching, we now turn our attention directly to the college professor.

Confronting Reluctance

Why is it that faculty are reluctant to attend to their own abilities and skills as instructional communicators? Consider these possible explanations that have been heard and discussed on many college campuses.

1. Some faculty rely on their past communication skills, which have gotten them through advanced degrees and at least twenty-five years of living. Such a record bespeaks communication habits that are well established, if not skills that are highly developed. These habits may need atten-

tion but are very hard to change. Recently, in my "Communication for Teachers" class, a student in her early twenties finished a teaching lesson for a group of twelve peers. Her own reaction to the lesson went as follows: "I knew I wasn't looking at one side of the room, but for some reason I just couldn't force myself to move my head. It would be like moving a concrete wall!" Habits do seem like brick walls, but with attention they can change.

2. Some faculty may be embarrassed to discuss or even acknowledge (whether to themselves or others) that their communication behaviors are less than satisfactory. One's communication behaviors are the means by which the self is presented to others; to discuss them is to touch on a very personal and sensitive issue—the self.

3. Some faculty may acknowledge the need for developing communication skills but cannot or will not commit the time and energy required to produce results. If they lack the required patience and perseverance in changing habits, old behaviors persist; the person could easily settle into complacency with those limited skills.

4. Some faculty may view even tactful suggestions about their teaching-communicating skills as an affront, an invasion of the privacy and personal nature of teaching and the teacher-student relationship. One's teaching style can then become off-limits to discussion.

5. Some faculty may have been trained to believe that, if they know their content, they will be able to communicate this information to others effectively. Many disciplines overlook the training of their future professors in the skills of teaching and communicating.

6. Some faculty may fear that the concerns they express about teaching effectively will be viewed by peers and superiors as a sign of inadequate subject matter preparation or competence. Such concern may actually be regarded as a drawback to achieving promotion and tenure.

7. Some faculty may consider the teaching-communicating end of their profession as unimportant or unnecessary. There may be a sense that it is the *student's* responsibility to adjust to the teacher's communication habits. Professors who demonstrate some degree of adjustment to the students, however, have noted positive effects on the climate of the class and the ability of teacher and students to work together. In my own teaching, I devote a class session during the first week of the course to one specific end: learning the names of every student and getting a sense of their interests, talents, and career goals. I use this information during the term to adjust examples, case studies, and course materials to the specific group, and the students gain a sense of working as a group rather than in isolation.

8. Some faculty may fear that non-traditional, more active, or energized teaching styles would be tagged by students and peers as "mere entertainment." If an instructor is entertaining at the expense of knowledge of the course, such criticism is justified. But when an instructor can be both entertaining and knowledgeable, engage both the students and the subject

matter, learning is surely being fostered. Eble referred to this situation when he wrote, "We spend too much time worrying about the deceit of acting, too little about the impact it enables one human being to have on another, too little on how much fun it is, for both the actor and audience" (1983, p. 9). Also underlying this fear may be the belief that such active teaching would display more of the teacher's person (self) and that such display is not appropriate to teaching.

9. Some faculty may wish to work on their instructional skills but are not supported either by colleagues or administrators. Perhaps there are no institutional norms or support for such instructional goals, no informed and interested colleagues with whom to confer, no footpaths established to meet these concerns.

The majority of the reasons cited suggest that there may be a social and professional stigma attached to college faculty who seek to improve their instructional communication. One's sense of professional priorities may be questioned by colleagues, chairpersons, or deans. But unless one is a "natural" teacher, it does take time and effort to develop and refine the means by which knowledge is shared with others—communication.

Conclusion

Just as audiences expect actors both to know the script and to bring it to life, so do students expect teachers both to know their subject and to communicate that knowledge. Unfortunately, our education system assumes communication skills to develop without training or attention. They key question involves the *degree of effectiveness* of the teaching and communicating. There is no disputing that teaching and communicating occur all around us every day. However, superior teaching and communicating (and acting) are less common, and they are special treats for those who come across them. Speaking is a natural developmental process; eloquence is an acquired skill. This superior quality does take care, nurturing, time, energy, and practice, but whether in teaching, communicating, or acting, it *is* worth the effort.

In an essay on "conscious teaching," John Granrose (1980) describes the "lesser and greater mysteries of teaching." The lesser mysteries are the basic skills of teaching: choosing, preparing, speaking, listening, responding, testing, and grading. One of the greater mysteries is that teaching is a "coming of age" and maturing process. It involves the recognition that others are also real people with their own hopes, dreams, and fears, deserving of one's respect and consideration. Finally, "inspired teaching" involves love of students and of self. Granrose concludes, "After all, to wake our students up, we ourselves must be awake; to inspire them, we ourselves must be inspired; to love them, we must be loved ourselves" (p. 29). In an essay on intrinsic motivation, Mihaly Czikszentmihalyi made a similar observation: "The most influential teachers . . . *are* usually the ones who love what they are doing, who show by their dedication and their passion that there is nothing else on earth they would rather be doing" (1982, pp. 19–20).

Communication is more than proper speaking skills. As evidenced by the writings in this volume, effective communication is the means by which we carry out our profession and express our attitudes about that profession and the students. Faculty can learn much from the practice of speaking and acting skills, but it must be remembered that teaching is not a mere act. Rather, it is an interact, a relationship. Performances in both the theater and the classroom become superior and inspired only when that relationship and the realness of the participants is acknowledged and communicated with finesse. Communication can then move from the lesser to the greater mysteries of teaching.

References

Bess, J. L. "The Motivation to Teach: Meanings, Messages, and Morals." In J. L. Bess (Ed.), *Motivating Professors to Teach Effectively.* New Directions for Teaching and Learning, no. 10. San Francisco: Jossey-Bass, 1982.

Czikszentmihalyi, M. "Intrinsic Motivation and Effective Teaching: A Flow Analysis." In J. L. Bess (Ed.), *Motivating Professors to Teach Effectively.* New Directions for Teaching and Learning, no. 10. San Francisco: Jossey-Bass, 1982.

Eble, K. E. *The Aims of College Teaching.* San Francisco: Jossey-Bass, 1982.

Granrose, J. T. "Conscious Teaching: Helping Assistants Develop Teaching Styles." In K. E. Eble (Ed.), *Improving Teaching Styles.* New Directions for Teaching and Learning, no. 1. San Francisco: Jossey-Bass, 1980.

Homan, S. "The Classroom as Theater." In J. Katz (Ed.), *Teaching as Though Students Mattered.* New Directions for Teaching and Learning, no. 21. San Francisco: Jossey-Bass, 1985.

Lowman, J. *Mastering the Techniques of Teaching.* San Francisco: Jossey-Bass, 1984.

Murray, H. G. "Classroom Teaching Behaviors Related to College Teaching Effectiveness." In J. G. Donald and A. M. Sullivan (Eds.), *Using Research to Improve Teaching.* New Directions for Teaching and Learning, no. 23. San Francisco: Jossey-Bass, 1985.

Rubin, R. B. (Ed.). *Improving Speaking and Listening Skills.* New Directions for College Learning Assistance, no. 12. San Francisco: Jossey-Bass, 1983.

Spitzberg, B. H., and Cupach, W. R. *Interpersonal Communication Competence.* Beverly Hills, Calif.: Sage, 1984.

Timpson, W. M., and Tobin, D. N. *Teaching as Performing.* Englewood Cliffs, N. J.: Prentice-Hall, 1982.

Jean M. Civikly is associate professor of Speech Communication at the University of New Mexico. In addition to her teaching and research on the interpersonal dynamics of instructional communication, she is director of the university's Teaching Assistant Resource Center.

In the college classroom culture, the norms for behavior and the values by which students are judged are largely extensions of mainstream Anglo culture.

The Ethnocentric Classroom

John C. Condon

Some years ago, I happened to ask a group of American and Japanese elementary school teachers to describe what kids did during class that really bothered them. An American teacher immediately volunteered that she was most disturbed when a child would tip back in his chair and rock unsteadily on two legs. There was immediate, spirited, and seemingly unanimous agreement among the teachers from both cultures. When, however, we discussed why that behavior was so upsetting, there emerged somewhat different interpretations for the two groups of teachers—patterns I have found consistently in the reactions of hundreds of teachers I have since asked. For the Americans, the first and strongest reaction is usually "the child might fall backwards and get hurt." (If asked about other concerns, "breaking the chair" is often mentioned.) Although the Japanese teachers readily understand that reaction, their primary concern is that the child is not acting properly as a student should, nor is the child showing the respect due the teacher. These feelings are certainly appreciated by the Americans, but they do not appear as primary concerns. Other differences in interpretation often emerge as well. Ask an American teacher why the child might be doing this, and common explanations are "boredom" or "too much energy." The Japanese teacher is more likely to share responsibility with the student: "If the child is not acting like a good student, it means I have not been a good teacher."

J. M. Civikly, (Ed.). *Communicating in College Classrooms.*
New Directions for Teaching and Learning, no. 26. San Francisco: Jossey-Bass, June 1986.

Several of the most fundamental considerations of cultural issues in the classroom, even the university classroom, are present in this simple example:

1. *Teacher expectations* concerning appropriate student behavior: "Students should not rock in their chairs."

2. *Student's actual behavior* may or may not correspond to those expectations (a child tips back in his chair). Note that often it is only when an expectation is *not* met that we recognize what our expectations are.

3. *Teacher feelings* (being upset) and the *bases for interpretations given for the reactions:* "I am worried he may get hurt," or, "I am upset because he is not showing respect."

4. *Teacher explanations for the deviant behavior:* "He is bored," or, "I have not adequately taught the child to act appropriately." These explanations, which may be characterized as *attributions,* are infused with cultural values—in this case the American's independent, individualistic concerns regarding the child putting himself in danger, and the Japanese concerns for interdependence, issues of situationally appropriate role behavior for the child, respect for the teacher and classroom, and even the teacher's own responsibility for the behavior. It is also possible that an American teacher would be as upset by the rudeness of the behavior as by the safety issue, but our cultural values still influence how we interpret even to ourselves our own reactions. If so, it may seem preferable for the American teacher to focus on the safety issue rather than on values related to respect and student role behavior.

5. *Teacher responses* may involve the child being reprimanded or reminded to behave, verbally or through action, in public or in private. These responses too will reflect the values, norms, and familiar behavior of one's culture. What calls for an immediate and emotional response in one culture may be but one of several options to consider in another.

Defining Culture

"Culture" is a useful abstraction representing all that we have learned and share with others. It informs and guides our behavior, how we interpret the behavior of others, and how we look at the world in general. Culture has to do with behaving according to what one learned was the norm ("acting normally") and reacting to behavior that in some way violates the norm. The irony is that we are not usually aware that our own culture has shaped our idea of "normal" until we encounter people whose upbringing has prepared them differently. Thus the advice about intercultural communication, "When in Rome . . . ," is at best only half of what is needed; one would need not only to *do* as the Romans do, but also to perceive and interpret the Roman's behavior as another Roman might. The Romans, of course, think they are just acting "naturally" or "normally."

A frequently quoted definition of culture put forth by anthropologist Ward Goodenough (1971) states all this quite simply: A culture consists of all that one must believe or know in order to act appropriately in any given situation. Obviously, not everyone from the same culture, or even from the same family for that matter, thinks and acts in exactly the same way. Despite this wide range of alternatives obvious to persons within a culture, outsiders would find it remarkably consistent.

Cultures and Classrooms

In culture in the sense described here, there are cultural issues to consider in every classroom. Even in those classrooms where the students appear to be homogeneous, a comparison of the teacher's and students' understanding of what is appropriate behavior will reveal some differences.

In addition to one's own upbringing, each teacher is part of an *academic culture*, which involves values, assumptions, and expectations regarding competition, verbal display, and classroom decorum, as well as a distinct style of speech within the classroom, and much more. Indeed, many American college teachers regard themselves as different in some ways from "ordinary" Americans, and perhaps even more feel that they are perceived by others as "different."

Distinctions are also made among academic disciplines. In his celebrated essay (1959), C. P. Snow argued that there were two cultures, of the sciences and the humanities, as different from each other as were two societies on opposite sides of an ocean. Eavesdropping on faculty conversations on any campus reveals that most disciplines are identified as "different from us," though perhaps not so different from us as are townspeople and state legislators. We often talk about such groupings as some people speak of persons whose ethnic backgrounds are seen as quite different. Still more distinctions can be identified for different institutions— there is a "Harvard culture," which is readily distinguished from, say, an "Antioch College culture." At what ethnographers would call the "microcultural" level, we find a set of values, norms, rituals, routine behavior, pacing, and language unique to each classroom. In fact, there are similarities between students encountering a new course and professor, and visitors entering a new society. Both experience "culture shock" to varying degrees, and both seem to cope in comparable ways. (The parallels are even more obvious for high-pressure professional schools, such as medicine or law.) Each student learns, with considerable initial stress, to modify past behavior, language, and manners to fit the new situation.

When the term "multicultural" is used in connection with classrooms, however, the emphasis is usually on cultural differences among students. This is particularly so when students come from varied national or ethnic backgrounds or from a wide age range, as with recent high school graduates and middle-aged returning students. Usually, teachers are aware of what they perceive as a cultural variation based on the student's physical appearance, style of clothing, or manner of speaking. *The more important considerations, of course, are those which are not so apparent: how the student has been taught to view the world and to act and react.* It is in this regard that the intercultural issues in the classroom come to the fore. It may be fair to say that most teachers regard their particular academic culture as the norm to which students from all backgrounds must adjust or be judged lacking. If we accept that we are a part of an academic culture, then most of us who are teachers are "ethnocentric" in the popular sense of that term. We take our ways as "normal" or "right" or even "the best of the alternatives we have known," and we are likely to feel very uncomfortable with and critical of student behavior that does not meet what we regard as appropriate norms. That, after all, is what it means to be a teacher—to proclaim, to foster, and ideally to model exemplary thought and communication in our particular fields, and to encourage and reward those who fulfill our hopes and discourage in one way or another those who do not.

But another consideration is far more important: the conjunction of the values and behavior of academic culture with those of the dominant cultural forces of this society—"middle-class/Anglo/mainstream American." The norms for behavior and the values by which students are judged in our classes are not just those of our particular field, institution, and the dynamics of a particular classroom. Rather, academic cultures in the United States today are to a great degree extensions of mainstream American culture. Students who come into the classroom from that background have a much easier time adjusting to the classroom culture than those whose backgrounds are different—including many inner-city Blacks, Native Americans, Hispanics, Southeast Asian refugee children, other ethnic minorities, and international students.

In so many respects, the classroom culture expresses what anthropologists and foreign observers alike have pointed to as very "American" values, assumptions, and ways of thinking. They appear in our textbooks, our syllabi, our topics for discussion, and often in the rationales given for the class itself. But perhaps most important of all, they appear in the interaction or communication that takes place in the classroom. Who is encouraged to speak, and how is this encouragement shown? Which interruptions are appropriate, and which are not? How much self-disclosure is appropriate in the public setting of a classroom? What conflict and confrontation styles are encouraged, and what styles create discomfort? If a student is corrected or criticized, is this done in front of others or individually? Many such questions about the norms of communication in the classroom can be—and should be—considered.

Culture and Communication

Anthropologists, notably Gregory Bateson (Ruesch and Bateson, 1951) and Edward Hall (1959), have remarked on the inseparability of patterns of a culture and patterns of communication within that culture: Describe one, and you invariably describe the other. Certainly, if we take a contemporary view of communication to include all behavior to which meaning is attached, we have an abbreviated definition of the culture. We can thus describe the classroom culture by describing classroom communication norms and patterns. We could similarly describe values, problem solving, patterns of thinking, and other relevant topics of classroom cultures. We would then be likely to find approximations of the values, preferred problem-solving methods, and patterns of thought that are identified with the mainstream Anglo-American culture.

In an influential article on Peace Corps training methods, Harrison and Hopkins (1967) compared values, assumptions, and communication patterns characteristic of American university classrooms with alternatives felt to be more appropriate to situations in the Third World countries in which Peace Corps volunteers may find themselves. The article has a new application here, for much of what the authors identify as more relevant for a Peace Corps volunteer in Ecuador, Nepal or Ghana would also be more relevant to many American ethnic minorities than is the mainstream Anglo "university model" they encounter. Highlights of the university model and relevant alternatives are presented below.

University Model	Alternative Model
Communication:	*Communication:*
To communicate fluently and directly via the written word and to a lesser extent, to speak well. To master the languages of abstraction and generalization, e.g., mathematics and science. To understand readily the reasoning, the ideas, and the knowledge of other persons through verbal exchange.	To understand and communicate directly and often nonverbally through movement, facial expression, and person-to-person actions. To listen with sensitivity to the hidden concerns, values, and motives of the other. To be at home in the exchange of feelings, attitudes, desires, and fears. To have a sympathetic, empathic understanding of the feelings of the other.
Problem Solving:	*Problem Solving:*
A problem is solved when the true, correct, reasonable answer has been discovered and verified. Problem solving is a search for knowledge and the truth. It is a largely rational process, involving intelligence, creativity, insight and a respect for facts.	A problem is solved when decisions are made and carried out which effectively apply people's energies to overcoming some barrier to a common goal. Problem solving is a social process, involving communication, interpersonal influence, consensus, and commitment.

University Model *(cont.)*	Alternative Model *(cont.)*
Source of Information:	*Source of Information:*
Information comes from experts and authoritative sources through the media of books, lectures, audiovisual presentations. "If you have a question, look it up."	Information sources must be developed by the learner from the social environment. Information-gathering methods include observation and questioning of associates, other learners, and chance acquaintances.
Role of Emotions and Values:	*Role of Emotions and Values:*
Problems are largely dealt with at an ideational level. Questions of reason and of fact are paramount. Feelings and values may be discussed but are rarely acted upon.	Problems are usually value- and emotion-laden. Facts are often less relevant than the perceptions and attitudes which people hold. Values and feelings have action consequences, and actions must be taken.

Source: Adapted from Harrison and Hopkins, 1967, pp. 435–438.

Compare these descriptions, written two decades ago for training Americans to go abroad, with more recent observations by Thomas Kochman (1981) on black and white interactions in American university classrooms. Kochman points out that a significant difference in the behavior of inner city black and white students is their emotional involvement in what they discuss. Blacks will often speak as advocates for a position, taking a stand on an issue, while white students are more likely to remain neutral and present "the facts." If a black student criticizes "the facts" or theory presented, the white student may well say, "Look, don't yell at me, I'm just telling you what so-and-so says." Should a black student challenge a white student, demanding to know the student's own point of view, the white student typically becomes defensive and says that his or her own point of view is not relevant or is no business of the questioner. Black students are likely to regard the white reaction with suspicion and disdain. In fact, what the white student is doing is showing that he or she has been adequately acculturated to the classroom, at least with respect to emotional involvement and objectivity. These norms and values had been modeled and taught in a dozen ways and thousands of times previously. Nor is impatience with the white student's refusal to take a stand peculiar to inner city blacks. I have seen comparable expressions of exasperations with "you Americans" or "you American academics" from English and Australian friends who find so many Americans unable to take a stand and defend it with passion and wit. Many Asians, on the other hand, find some American social conversations too confrontational and therefore unpleasant. They may describe the American as immature in his or her relative lack of emotional control. Teachers who are acculturated to the university model are likely to respond nervously to such an exchange, possibly attributing motives arising from personal hostility rather than cultural norms and values for the exchange of ideas. Similarly, some Native American students are reluctant to speak in class or call attention to their personal views, they may be judged by Anglo norms as shy, uninterested, or even unprepared, rather than by their own culture's norms and values concerning the appropriateness of speech and self-effacement.

Curiously, many academics who immediately see the importance of teaching Peace Corps volunteers about values, assumptions, norms of communication, and other culture-related matters may not realize that comparable learning is necessary in their own classrooms, where nearly every group is to some degree multicultural. The more common view, I fear, is ethnocentric: What is normal for me should be the norm for everyone as long as they are in my class.

Values and Teaching

If we turn to values identified with mainstream culture in the U.S. today, we find that these too are deeply embedded in all that goes on in the classroom. Such values include independence, individualism, competition, pragmatic concern for relevance and application, impatience with too much theory or too few concrete examples, attention to the near past and near future, optimism about the goodness of human nature and the potential for improving, a dispassionate attitude that nature may be restructured to conform to immediate social agendas, trust in technologies, and so on. Our reasoning patterns greatly favor the inductive and the analytic, and our rhetoric encourages the non-intimate and non-formal.

To illustrate the place of values, consider briefly the values of independence and individualism—those perhaps most often said to characterize Americans (usually meaning mainstream Americans). Group activities are not uncommon, but the groups tend to be organized only for the purpose and duration of the activity. "Helping" another, as in whispering the correct answer during recitations in a language class, is not encouraged or tolerated. For many students, expecting no help seems perfectly natural. A lifetime of experiences has given value to independence and individualism: having one's own room and private possessions, doing one's own chores, for which one receives one's own allowance. For others, including immigrant and refugee young people from Asia as well as cultures that value interdependence, such as traditional Native Americans, the line between academic individualism and insensitivity may be difficult to discern.

To paraphrase what Hall said so well (1959, p. 39), a culture conceals more than it reveals—ironically, it conceals itself most of all from its own people. Were this not the case, teachers might be able to lay out for students on the very first day the assumptions, expectations, and values that shape the course and the teacher's judgment of all a student would do. The formal requirements of a course can be and usually are presented in some detail, but the informal and tacit expectations of the classroom culture, including the norms of interpersonal communication, are beyond the conscious awareness of most teachers.

There is yet another problem concerning culture, classrooms, and communication: that of ambiguity. Perhaps nearly every culture that helps to make up U.S. society today faces ambiguities about values, beliefs, sex roles, authority, and much more. Students are likely to enter the classroom with uncertainties and mixed feelings about their values and goals. A young Hispanic woman who is the first in her family to go to a university may be excited about becoming a career woman and gaining success through competition with men and women; at the same time, she feels pressure from home not to be too assertive or to forget her role as daughter and her family's expectations that she will marry and raise a family. Then she enters the classroom culture, which presents its own set of ambiguities: "Speak out, your opinion is important. You will be graded on participation. But, don't speak too long or off the subject or otherwise violate the class norms. I am a facilitator of discussion, for your opinions matter. I am now stating my opinion, but it is just my opinion, and not necessarily what the experts say. You may be tested on this."

Teachers also find themselves—or place themselves—in ambiguous relationships with students, much as parents have with their children. On the one hand, many teachers encourage students to discuss and even to disagree with the teacher. Students are likely to be told that their opinions matter, and even that they have as much to offer as the teacher does. It is not uncommon for students to have some say in routine class procedures such as the scheduling of an examination. Titles are used less and often with some awkwardness in feeling either too formal or too informal. Even personal names may be used as forms of address, without any intent of showing disrespect. On the other hand, most teachers maintain and demonstrate their superior position by showing approval and disapproval in comments and in grading—ways that students cannot employ. Teachers may want to serve as facilitators of a process of discussion, but in subtle ways their reactions to student comments help to signal their own view on the topic at hand.

The point here is that the familiar role of a teacher in an American university is confusing to students from a variety of backgrounds. Just as many students from abroad and from more traditional cultures within the U.S. express shock at "how children treat their parents here," many are surprised by what they find in classrooms. An Egyptian student once said to me, "Yesterday you came to class a few minutes late and apologized. Five minutes later a student came to class and didn't apologize. Everything is backwards here!" The Egyptian student's comment amused me and also informed me about my behavior and expectations. I do apologize when late, partly for personal reasons but also because of my cultural background. It is one of many small ways in which many American teachers attempt to reduce the difference in status between themselves and their students, in the belief that this fosters better communication and thus increases the likelihood of learning. At the same time, it can be puzzling to students who expect a clearly marked difference in status.

Students also have culturally based ambiguities about appropriate classroom behavior. In a class of fifty students, I once wanted to show a film and had trouble getting the projector to work. I asked if there was anyone in the class who could help. No one volunteered, which I took to mean that no one knew any more about the machine than I did. After a few minutes, one young man, and then a woman seated next to him, came to help, and the problem was corrected. A few days later, the man who had helped out wrote a note about the experience. He wrote that he had wanted to volunteer immediately but had not wanted to appear to the other students as trying to impress the teacher. He supposed that others in the class might have had similar feelings. The student had been caught between a personal desire to help and counterpressures from a classroom culture. Had the same situation occurred in another society where the expressed difference in status of the teacher is more sharply distinguished, more students might have volunteered to help without a second thought, since "helping the teacher" is part of the shared expectations for students in many other cultures.

Conclusion

Most of what teachers value, expect, and encourage through the communication that occurs in their classes is apart from the formal requirements of the course or the teacher's consciousness. Ethnographers who study classroom cultures sometimes refer to this as "the hidden curriculum" (Gearing and Epstein, 1982). To a considerable degree, that "curriculum" is at the heart of communication in the university classroom. It reflects the teacher's personal and academic cultural background, which in turn is strongly influenced by the dominant cultural system in the society. To be more aware of one's own cultural assumptions and behavior is to resist making negative judgments of students from very different backgrounds when their behavior does not conform to one's expectations. By recognizing that what is common in "common sense" is what is shared in common with others from one's culture, one can resist some of those cultural pressures and so alter one's choices and actions.

References

Gearing, F. and Epstein, P. "Learning to Wait: An Ethnographic Probe into the Operations of an Item of Hidden Curriculum." In G. Spindler (Ed.), *Doing the Ethnography of Schooling: Educational Anthropology in Action.* New York: Holt, Rinehart and Winston, 1982.

Goodenough, W. *Culture, Language and Society.* Reading, Mass.: Addison-Wesley, 1971.

Hall, E. T. *The Silent Language.* Garden City, N.Y.: Doubleday, 1959.

Harrison, R., and Hopkins, R. "The Design of Cross-Cultural Training: An Alternative to the University Model." *Journal of Applied Behavioral Science,* 1967, *3,* 431–460.

Kochman, T. *Black and White Styles in Conflict.* Chicago: University of Chicago Press, 1981.

Ruesch, J. and Bateson, G. *Communication: Social Matrix of Psychiatry.* New York: Norton, 1951.

Snow, C. P. *The Two Cultures.* Cambridge: Cambridge University Press, 1959.

John C. Condon is professor of Speech Communication at the University of New Mexico, specializing in intercultural communication. His most recent books are With Respect to the Japanese: A Guide for Americans *(1984), and* Good Neighbors: Communicating with the Mexicans *(1985).*

Communication is critical to success in academic, occupational and social settings. Communication apprehension adversely affects this success.

Communication Apprehension in the College Classroom

John A. Daly

Anyone who spends time in the classroom recognizes that students differ in their propensities to engage in, and enjoy, communicating. Some seem to savor any opportunity for verbal activity; they like to talk and seek out chances to be heard. These students always seem ready with answers to questions or comments about class material and visibly enjoy activities such as group discussions and oral presentations. At the other extreme are students, sometimes labeled as shy, reticent, or communication-apprehensive, who dislike and even fear communicating. These students never seem to answer questions aloud, prefer working alone on projects, and often remain virtually unnoticed by teachers and fellow students. This tendency for some students to enjoy communicating and for others to dislike the activity is the focus of research known as *communication apprehension.*

    Communication apprehension is an individual difference in inclination of individuals to seek out and enjoy communication. At one extreme are low apprehensives—people who like communicating and find it rewarding; at the other extreme are high apprehensives—people who dislike and fear communicating. High apprehensive people find commu-

J. M. Civikly, (Ed.). *Communicating in College Classrooms.*
New Directions for Teaching and Learning, no. 26. San Francisco: Jossey-Bass, June 1986.

nication more punishing than rewarding. Communication apprehension may be manifested in a variety of ways, some behavioral, others cognitive, but whatever the indicator, those with low apprehension differ in many respects from those with high apprehension. Some distinctions may help in understanding this construct.

The first distinction is between transitory (state) communication apprehension and dispositional (trait) apprehension. Transitory apprehension is the temporary nervousness or anxiety an individual might feel in a particular situation. At the start of a speech, for instance, most people feel some tremors of nervousness, as they also do when starting an important job interview. Dispositional or trait apprehension, on the other hand, is not tied to a specific communication event. People with high dispositional apprehension generally feel nervous and uncomfortable in any setting where communication is required. In situations that would normally elicit some degree of transitory anxiety, people high in dispositional communication apprehension experience significantly more anxiety than their low apprehensive counterparts.

A second distinction lies in the media involved in the communication activity. There is a good amount of research on two types of apprehension: oral communication apprehension (Daly and McCroskey, 1984) and writing apprehension (Daly, 1985). Far less work has focused on receiver apprehension (Wheeless, 1975) and singing apprehension (Andersen and others, 1978). Each type focuses on the anxiety an individual feels toward some form of communication. Although the emphasis in this chapter will be on *oral* communication apprehension (henceforth called just "communication apprehension" for simplicity's sake), it is important to remember that there are other apprehensions.

The third distinction is one of context. In recent work, scholars have suggested that individuals vary in their degree of communication apprehension in different situations. Four major contexts have been identified: public (formal speaking), meeting (department gatherings), group (small discussion activities), and dyadic (one-to-one conversations). An individual might be a high public communication apprehensive, but only moderately apprehensive in small group and dyadic contacts.

Why focus on communication apprehension in the classroom? There are two very important reasons. First, high communication apprehension is widespread. Some scholars have suggested that close to 20% of the U.S. population may suffer from degrees of apprehension sufficient to prevent them from successfully communicating in the manner they wish. Second, evidence indicates that apprehension profoundly affects how people communicate, and communication is critical to success in academic settings as well as virtually all other environments. Our society as a whole, and the academic world in particular, values sociability. Many instructors include class participation in their grading schemes; many require oral reports; some assess learning by oral questioning; and most regard with favor those students who show their attentiveness and involvement by questions, comments, suggestions, and requests. Students who like communicating fare better in the classroom than those who do not.

Correlates and Consequences of Communication Apprehension

There has been extensive research on communication apprehension in the past fifteen years (Daly and McCroskey, 1984). The research can be categorized into two broad clusters. The first emphasizes general characteristics and consequences of apprehension; the second focuses on the role of apprehension in classroom settings.

General Characteristics and Consequences. As a general conclusion, research on communication apprehension suggests that the more apprehensive an individual is, the less positively others regard him or her. High apprehensives are perceived to be less socially attractive, friendly, attentive, responsive, and assertive than low apprehensives. In conversations, others perceive high apprehensives as less involved and more tense, inhibited, and unfriendly than their more outgoing low apprehensive counterparts. Moreover, high apprehensive individuals tend to have lower positive regard for themselves than their counterparts. Greater apprehension is related to greater loneliness, lower self-esteem, less positive self-evaluation for performances, and a tendency to be less argumentative, assertive, or dominant.

Behaviorally, people high in communication apprehension, when compared to low apprehensives, tend to talk with less frequency, offer more irrelevant comments in discussion, interrupt less often, have longer pauses before responding in conversations, make more negative statements about themselves, offer more submissive statements in group interactions, disclose less about themselves, and make more errors when asked to recall their conversations. In social relationships, high apprehensive people tend to date fewer people, have fewer friends, and be more conforming. In occupational settings, high apprehensive individuals are less likely to fare well in interviews or to succeed in managerial jobs where personnel management is important and are more likely to select jobs that demand little communication. The problem for high apprehensives is that many positions having high status, and certainly many that are materially rewarded, go to those who enjoy and seek out communication opportunities. High apprehensive people do just the opposite and seldom reap society's rewards. (See Chapter 2 of this volume for relevant insights on culture and communication in the classroom.)

Classroom Correlates. In classroom settings, high apprehensive students perceive their teachers as less animated, dramatic, friendly, open, and immediate. Teachers have similar reactions to them, having less positive expectations for students whom they view as high in apprehension. In studies using hypothetical prototypes of high and low apprehensive pupils, teachers rate the low apprehensive students more positively in terms of anticipated performance in a variety of courses and also more likely to succeed in school. Research using actual students who differ in apprehension levels supports the finding that teachers have a positive bias towards low apprehensive pupils. Within classrooms, high apprehensives prefer traditional seating arrangements to ones that enhance teacher-student interaction (for example, horseshoe arrangements) and will choose seats where they are less noticed by teachers and pupils.

Research consistently finds little or no relationship between intelligence and apprehension. However, if educational achievement and performance are considered rather than intellectual ability, communication apprehension is relevant. McCroskey and Andersen (1976) demonstrated a significant relationship between communication apprehension and scores on standardized tests such as the ACT (American College Testing program). They also found that extremely high apprehensives have, on average, a significantly lower college grade point average than do extremely low apprehensives. Other researchers have found that low apprehensive college students receive significantly higher grades on assignments in communication-related courses than high apprehensive students.

Development of Communication Apprehension

There has been some interest in exploring the ways in which individuals develop communication apprehension (Van Kleeck and Daly, 1982). Detailing the different ways communication apprehension can develop helps one understand how it may be created in the classroom, as well as how it may be reduced. Four explanations have been proposed.

The first explanation is a genetic one. There is good evidence to suggest that peoples' levels of general sociability are, to some extent, genetically based (Buss and Plomin, 1984). There is little that can be done to modify the genetic make-up of an individual, but the degree to which genetics contributes directly to apprehension is likely to be minor.

The second explanation emphasizes the critical role played by reinforcement. This thesis holds that high apprehensives have a history of being punished for their communication attempts, while their low apprehensive counterparts have typically been rewarded. High apprehensives have learned over time that communication is punishing, and they withdraw from situations that demand communicating.

The third explanation is inadequate skill development. The hypothesis is that high apprehensives have failed to develop communication skills as quickly and as well as low apprehensives. It is not simply having inadequate skills. More important may be the relative rate of acquisition of the skills. Children who develop communication skills later than most are at a disadvantage among their peers. Punishments from peers for having inadequate skills probably increase the apprehension of the child.

The fourth explanation emphasizes the critical role of adequate communication models. High apprehensive individuals may be so because they have not been exposed to role models that are as good as those seen by low apprehensives. The research base for this explanation lies in studies demonstrating that social isolation in children often can be reduced by exposing them to videotapes of highly sociable children engaging in social activities.

The latter three explanations taken together create a vicious circle for high apprehensives. Because of their history of delayed skills development and inadequate models high apprehensives would not succeed as well in communication attempts as low apprehensives. Given this lack of success, they probably would not continue to expose themselves to communication activities, thus further reducing the practice that enhances skill development.

Measuring Communication Apprehension

Since communication apprehension has a number of consequences both outside and inside the classroom, the question arises as to how one might measure a student's degree of apprehension. There are two ways. The first is through systematic observation of students' behavior. A number of methods are available (Mulac and Wiemann, 1984). For example, a teacher might create a chart plotting the general pattern of classroom communication for each student—how much each one talks each day over some period of time, how often each volunteers answers, how active each is in class discussions, and so on. While one would not anticipate a one-to-one relationship between each behavior and apprehension, it could be expected that the overall pattern of a student's verbal behavior would be a rough indicator of apprehension.

A second approach is through self-report measures of apprehension. The underlying assumption of self-report measures is that respondents know how they feel about the topic being addressed by the questionnaire. In the case of communication apprehension, there are a wide variety of measures available to the classroom instructor. Most are brief, requiring little more than a few minutes of class time. By and large, they have good reliability and validity. The most popular form was devised by James McCroskey and is titled the Personal Report of Communication Apprehension (PRCA). He and Virginia Richmond have recently published a book that contains a number of instruments for assessing apprehension (Richmond and McCroskey, 1985). A typical questionnaire is presented in Table 1.

26

Table 1. A Measure of Communication Apprehension

For each of the statements, please indicate the degree to which you (1) strongly agree, (2) agree, (3) are undecided, (4) disagree, or (5) strongly disagree.

 1. I dislike participating in group discussions. 1 2 3 4 5
 2. Generally, I am comfortable while participating in a group discussion. 1 2 3 4 5
 3. I am tense and nervous while participating in a group discussion. 1 2 3 4 5
 4. I like to get involved in group discussions. 1 2 3 4 5
 5. Engaging in a group discussion with new people makes me tense and nervous. 1 2 3 4 5
 6. I am calm and relaxed while participating in group discussions. 1 2 3 4 5
 7. Generally, I am nervous when I have to participate in a meeting. 1 2 3 4 5
 8. Usually I am calm and relaxed while participating in meetings. 1 2 3 4 5
 9. I am very calm and relaxed when I am called upon to express an opinion at a meeting. 1 2 3 4 5
10. I am afraid to express myself at meetings. 1 2 3 4 5
11. Communicating at meetings usually makes me uncomfortable. 1 2 3 4 5
12. I am very relaxed when answering questions at a meeting. 1 2 3 4 5
13. While participating in a conversation with a new acquaintance, I feel very nervous. 1 2 3 4 5
14. I have no fear of speaking up in conversations. 1 2 3 4 5
15. Ordinarily I am very tense and nervous in conversations. 1 2 3 4 5
16. Ordinarily I am very calm and relaxed in conversations. 1 2 3 4 5
17. While conversing with a new acquaintance, I feel very relaxed. 1 2 3 4 5
18. I'm afraid to speak up in conversations. 1 2 3 4 5
19. I have no fear of giving a speech. 1 2 3 4 5
20. Certain parts of my body feel very tense and rigid while giving a speech. 1 2 3 4 5
21. I feel relaxed while giving a speech. 1 2 3 4 5
22. My thoughts become confused and jumbled when I am giving a speech. 1 2 3 4 5
23. I face the prospect of giving a speech with confidence. 1 2 3 4 5
24. While giving a speech I get so nervous, I forget facts I really know. 1 2 3 4 5

This questionnaire allows you to compute a total score and four subscores. The subscores are for (1) group discussions, (2) meetings, (3) dyadic interactions, and (4) public speaking. You compute each by using the following:

Group discussion 18 + scores for items 2, 4, and 6;
 − scores for items 1, 3, and 5.

Meetings 18 + scores for items 8, 9, and 12;
 − scores for items 7, 10, and 11.

Dyadic 18 + scores for items 14, 16, and 17;
 − scores for items 13, 15, and 18.

Public speaking 18 + scores for items 19, 21, and 23;
 − scores for items 20, 22, and 24.

Your total score would simply be the sum of the four subscores. Your total score should fall between 24 and 120.

Source: Richmond and McCroskey, 1985. Reprinted by permission.

Modifying Communication Apprehension

Since high communication apprehension is not something most people seek as a trait, we are left with the question of how one might go about modifying an individual's apprehension (Glaser, 1981). There are two general approaches to the treatment of communication apprehension. The first is through behavioral therapies offered by trained therapists in communication or psychology. One of the most commonly used is *systematic desensitization*. The assumption behind this therapy is that high apprehensive people link the thought of some communication encounter with anxiety. The goal of systematic desensitization is to tie thoughts of communication to relaxation rather than to anxiety. In a comfortable setting, a therapist, after making sure the individuals are relaxed, asks them to visualize communication encounters. Any time they feel tense when thinking of an event they are told to concentrate on relaxing. Over time, thoughts of communication events are associated with relaxation rather than nervousness. Another therapy is *cognitive restructuring*. The assumption is that people suffering from high apprehension have unrealistic or dysfunctional beliefs about themselves and communication. They may say things like, "No one will like my performance," or, "I'm always the worst person in groups." The therapist's task is to challenge these beliefs logically and replace them with a set of beliefs that are both more realistic and more positive.

The second treatment approach seeks to change the contextual characteristics that tend to make people feel anxious. Some simple behavioral changes can, at the very least, make people more comfortable in communication settings, if not erase their apprehension. The basic theme of this approach is that most people who encounter high apprehensives are not professionally trained to change their apprehension. Instead, the best they can do is make the apprehensive's environment as comfortable as possible. Let me provide a few classroom examples of the sorts of things a teacher might do to aid students with communication apprehension. Underlying these strategies is an assumption that the classroom environment should be as supportive as possible for high apprehensives. When characteristics of the classroom or the teacher's instructional strategies needlessly increase students' apprehension, their academic performance is likely to suffer.

First, oral participation should not be required in classrooms where oral performances are only a means to an end rather than an end in and of themselves. In most classrooms, when teachers use class participation, the ability to answer questions aloud, or oral reports, they are not actually interested in students' competence in oral communication. What they want to know is whether pupils know and understand class materials. There are many ways of accomplishing this, only one of which is a reliance on oral participation. Indeed, by using oral activities to assess students, teachers may actually be missing their intended goal. There are countless stories of high apprehensive students who fare poorly in classes as diverse as English literature, mathematics, and art history simply because their oral participation is not up to par. They may know as much as or more than their peers who are low apprehensive, but their presentation of that knowledge is confounded by their apprehension. Consider the case of oral reading: Every year first graders throughout the country are placed in reading groups based, in part, upon teachers' perceptions of their reading abilities. A child's assignment to a particular group is critical to his or her future academic success. How do most teachers assess a child's reading ability? They judge by an oral performance. The problem is that a shy child, when faced with this task, may not perform well even though he or she may be a good reader. The same applies in college. Teachers are sometimes amazed to discover that a student who never seems to participate in class activities does incredibly well on written tests and papers. Teachers who reflect on this will probably come to understand that an individual's willingness to talk in class is not a good indicator of what he or she actually knows. Don't misunderstand: If it is the responsibility of the teacher to teach and assess oral communication competence, as in a speech class or foreign language course, participation is a reasonable demand. But most teachers, especially at the college level, do not have that as part of their academic mandate. There are other ways to assess knowledge and learning than oral renditions.

A second strategy is to let students sit where they want in classrooms. Seating students in alphabetical order, or in any other formal way, presents problems to the apprehensive student. Too often, the apprehensive student is placed front-and-center in the classroom, just where he or she will feel most uncomfortable. (Likewise, the low apprehensive may be placed far in the back, just where he or she will be unhappy.) A better approach is to let students select their own seats. Most likely, high apprehensives will select seats where they can listen and where attention will not be drawn to them. If assigned seating is used for attendance purposes, have students select their own seats before making the seating chart.

Teachers also need to be very cautious about their preconceptions regarding communication. Teachers who enter class with beliefs such as "Silence is golden" and "Students should not ask questions" often manage their classrooms accordingly: Quietness is reinforced and talkativeness punished. Over time, it is possible that teachers actually create apprehension. Students who feel that talk is something to be avoided because it is not favored by the teacher are likely to become apprehensive, at least in the class setting. Moreover, teachers need to exert a good deal of caution when dealing with students' communication activities. There are far too many cases of teachers ridiculing students' attempts at communication, demanding absolute quiet in their classrooms, or indiscriminately punishing talk. Students are close observers of teachers' reactions. When they see a teacher reacting negatively or apathetically to something, they tend to adapt to that teacher. When the adaptation is avoiding communication, apprehension can follow.

Public Speaking Anxiety as a Special Problem

One of the more common problems encountered by students and teachers alike is public speaking anxiety. When asked to address an audience of peers or students, many people feel unnaturally nervous and uncomfortable. Lecturing to classes, making conference presentations, or addressing faculty bodies are fundamental to the profession of college teaching. Yet many faculty members experience stage fright when doing so. Sometimes the stage fright becomes so extreme that the person is incapable of continuing his or her presentation. Why do people experience stage fright, and what can they do to reduce it?

Research and theory (Daly, 1984) suggest a number of reasons for stage fright. They include evaluation, novelty, conspicuousness, audience, and rules. The greater the perceived stakes the more likely people are to experience stage fright. Most people fear being evaluated, and one setting where evaluation is always present is the public speaking arena. Novel settings and experiences generally induce anxiety. For most people public speaking is a novel event, fraught with ambiguity and unfamiliarity. Beginning lecturers typically experience more stage fright than experienced ones—the novelty of lecturing wears off. When addressing an audience, one is also particularly conspicuous, as all eyes are on the speaker. Increased levels of conspicuousness are associated with elevated anxiety. This is so, in part, because when people feel conspicuous they become more self-focused. Decreased attention to one's audience often leads to less effective presentations, which, in turn, creates even more anxiety. Audience characteristics can also contribute to public speaking anxiety. How well speakers know their audiences, as well as the heterogeneity of audience members' backgrounds and personal characteristics, all make for difficulty in adapting materials to the listeners. This ambiguity often arouses anxiety. Finally, people experiencing stage fright often rely too much on rules about public speaking. They have overlearned a set of maxims about public speaking which, in the end, hinders their performances. Believing that one needs to have an excellent introduction, must be humorous, must be perfectly organized, and must not use unnecessary gestures are examples of rules that many anxious speakers hold sacred. These rules are likely to help speakers if they are viewed as general guidelines that can be followed when helpful and ignored when necessary. Taken to a rigid extreme, they often block successful presentations.

Overcoming stage fright is difficult, but there are some techniques experienced speakers use. These include preparation, relabeling arousal, audience focus, understanding audience perceptions, and forecasting. Preparation is an important key to effective presentations because it reduces the novelty of the situation. Speakers who select familiar topics and practice their presentations ahead of time generally experience less stage fright than persons who fail to prepare adequately. In classrooms, as in other settings, it is probably best to be overprepared. For some people, a public speaking situation is accompanied by great physical activation. This physical arousal can be called fear or stage fright, or it might be labeled excitement and anticipation. The physical manifestations are often the same. It is the psychological label attached to the experience that shapes the feelings a person experiences. Experienced speakers know that physical activation accompanying speeches can be reduced by exercises such as deep breathing and muscle relaxation before the presentation. Good speakers learn very early that one way of reducing anxiety is to focus their entire attention on the audience. They force themselves to think constantly about their audience, not themselves. The moment speakers start thinking about themselves—how they are sounding, how they look, how they are coming across—they are likely to start experiencing stage fright. Self-focused attention increases one's sense of being conspicuous, which is very often detrimental to speaking. Stage fright can also be lessened by understanding that most speakers are their own harshest critics. Research has shown that speakers often report feeling a great deal more anxiety than audience members perceive. Speakers also tend to be more negative about their performances than audiences are. These misperceptions, typically negative ones, can lead to stage fright. A final technique is to forecast problems. In every speaking event, something can go wrong: A microphone won't work; time allocations may change; agenda topics are changed; and so forth. Speakers who are prepared for any eventuality are less likely to experience stage fright.

Conclusion

Communication is central to learning. It is the medium of dispensing information, and it is the way of assessing much of what is learned. When students do not enjoy communicating, their opportunities for learning are restricted. When teachers fail to communicate or to understand why their students hold back from communicating, opportunities for learning are lost. The interaction necessary to effective teaching and learning diminishes when the students' anxieties are aroused. Research and theory about communication apprehension offer the classroom teacher ways of understanding and dealing with this important barrier to learning.

References

Andersen, P. A., Andersen, J. F., and Garrison, J. P. "Singing Apprehension and Talking Apprehension: The Development of Two Constructs." *Sign Language Studies,* 1978, *19,* 155-186.

Buss, A., and Plomin, R. *Temperament: Early Developing Personality Traits.* Hillsdale, N.J.: L. Erlbaum, 1984.

Daly, J. A. "Understanding and Overcoming Stage Fright." In J. L. Whitehead (Ed.), *Readings for Business and Professional Communication.* Lexington, Mass.: Ginn, 1984.

Daly, J. A. "Writing Apprehension." In M. Rose (Ed.), *Writing blocks.* New York: Guilford Press, 1985.

Daly, J. A., and McCroskey, J. C. (Eds.), *Avoiding Communication: Shyness, Reticence, and Communication Apprehension.* Beverly Hills, Calif.: Sage, 1984.

Glaser, S. R. "Oral Communication Apprehension and Avoidance: The Current Status of Treatment Research." *Communication Education,* 1981, *30,* 321-341.

McCroskey, J. C., and Andersen, J. "The Relationship Between Communication Apprehension and Academic Achievement Among College Students." *Human Communication Research,* 1976, *3,* 73-81.

Mulac, A., and Wiemann, J. "Observer Perceived Communicator Anxiety." In J. A. Daly and J. C. McCroskey (Eds.), *Avoiding Communication: Shyness, Reticence, and Communication Apprehension.* Beverly Hills, Calif.: Sage, 1984.

Richmond, V. P., and McCroskey, J. C. *Communication: Apprehension, Avoidance, and Effectiveness.* Scottsdale, Ariz.: Gorsuch Scarisbrick, 1985.

Van Kleeck, A., and Daly, J. A. "Instructional Communication Research and Theory: Communication Development and Instructional Communication." In M. Burgoon (Ed.), *Communication Yearbook 5.* New Brunswick, N.J.: Transaction Books, 1982.

Wheeless, L. R. "An Investigation of Receiver Apprehension and Social Context Dimensions of Communication Apprehension." *Speech Teacher,* 1975, *24,* 261-268.

John A. Daly is associate professor in the Department of
Speech Communication at the University of Texas at Austin.
He is currently editor of the quarterly journal
Communication Education *and co-editor of the quarterly*
Written Communication.

Beyond entertainment, teaching style shapes students'
critical focus.

Communicator Style in Teaching: Giving Good Form to Content

Robert W. Norton

While I greatly admire Kenneth Eble's book, *The Craft of Teaching: A Guide to Mastering the Professor's Art* (1976), it is his essay on teaching styles in an earlier volume of *New Directions for Teaching and Learning* (1980) that has provoked me to further study of the connections between teaching style and communicator style.

I agree with Eble that: (1) style in university teaching needs to be better respected by the teachers themselves; (2) style should not be confused with affectation; (3) style should not be denigrated as a kind of posturing to mask a lack of substance; and (4) style is not merely the natural manifestation of personal eccentricities.

In my view, however, it is necessary to introduce more precision in discussing the notion of teaching styles. For the educational researcher, the primary criteria with which to judge a definition of style are (1) whether the definition is at the appropriate level of abstraction and (2) whether the definition can be used to generate useful units of analysis.

J. M. Civikly, (Ed.). *Communicating in College Classrooms.*
New Directions for Teaching and Learning, no. 26. San Francisco: Jossey-Bass, June 1986.

Levels of Abstraction

The broadest definition of style, and consequently the least useful, is "the way something is done." For our purposes, four levels of style can be readily identified. First, the style of a person is the way character and personality are manifested. Second, the communicator style of the person at the macro level is the way he or she signals how literal meaning should be taken, filtered, or understood. Third, the communicator style at the micro level is the collection of nonverbal micro-momentary behaviors used by the individual. Finally, the teaching style of the person is the way he or she teaches. At each of these levels, behaviors are displayed and perceived differently.

The whole of a person's character is not manifested only by the way he or she communicates. The style of a person entails more than interaction patterns. In like manner, the teaching style of an individual is not identical to his or her communicator style. Teaching style is but one facet of the person's whole repertoire of communicating.

I was fascinated by Axelrod's (1980) profile of a college professor's career from 1959 to 1984. Over a period of twenty-five years, the professor shifted his teaching style from discussion leader to trainer of minds to intense caretaker to authority figure. The teaching style reflected the mood of the culture. In Axelrod's book, the transient nature of teaching styles left the professor pessimistic and confused.

Unlike personality and character, a person's teaching style changes as a function of student culture, societal mood, and shifting values. Teaching style is also affected by size of classes, type of subject, and level of students; a good teacher, like a good speaker, adapts to an audience.

Probably the most resistant level of style is that of personality and character, though change *is* possible. The next most resistant level of style is the way the person communicates; communication patterns are strongly habituated.

Units of Analysis

Because the levels of style have different qualities, it should be expected that what constitutes evidence of an effective teaching style varies. Table 1 shows what might constitute evidence for each level. While Eble focuses on character and the "style of person" level, my preference is to concentrate on the level of "communicator style" and to focus on the pragmatic. I assume that a person's overall pattern of communicating will manifest itself in the classroom regardless of other constraints. It would be interesting in future research, however, to compare a teacher's most general pattern of communication to the pattern by the classroom, types of students, topic, and levels of students.

Table 1. Units of Analysis for Respective Levels of Style

Style Level	Potential Units of Analysis
Style of person	*Personality perspectives:* (1) Social and cultural determinants of behavior, (2) organismic approach emphasizing purposeful human behavior, (3) personality structure, heredity, and biological determinants of behavior (Wiggins, 1973).
	Character perspectives: Temperament, virtue, morality, ethics, principles, etc.
Communicator style	*Macro level:* Consistently recurring association of pattern of communication (dramatic, dominant, open, animated, relaxed, attentive, friendly, etc.).
	Micro level: Form giving pattern for any given interaction (signals which have a pragmatic impact in shaping perception of literal message).
Teaching style	The recurring association of a teacher in a given class (large lecture, seminar, small class) for a given topic for a given level of students.

According to the *New Columbia Encyclopedia,* style is "the mysterious yet recognizable result of a successful blending of form with content." The many nuances of communication style found in social science and humanities literature can be reduced to two perspectives, which are inextricably connected (Norton, 1983). First, style is a form determinant: It signals how the message should be interpreted. Second, style is the consistently recurring association of the form-giving patterns. The rest of this chapter elaborates on these two perspectives.

Style as Form Giving

The first perspective on communicator style focuses on the way the person communicates any given message. The person signals the form in which a literal message is to be taken, filtered, or understood. The signals establish boundaries on how a message is to be processed and, conversely, how it should not be processed. Style is thus a form determinant. It represents the way something is distinguished: "Style is a message about content" (Norton, 1983, p. 19). In this sense, style has a pragmatic effect. In the context of the classroom, "style probably not only affects feelings toward the teacher and the class, but also influences learning. Style affects the *way* the teacher emphasizes material, organizes ideas, provides crucial focus, and sorts the trivial from the critical" (Norton, 1983, p. 53).

How, then, can an effective teacher give form (style) to content? Consider two physics teachers who want the students to understand that a mass at the end of a pendulum cannot gain energy in the swing. The first teacher states this point in the lecture, citing the appropriate mathematical evidence from various equations. The second teacher chooses to give form to the content in a different way: This teacher provides a dramatic frame. In the front of the room, there is a twenty-foot pendulum with a bowling ball as the mass. The teacher raises the bowling ball to the student's face and tells him not to move as the bowling ball comes swinging back along the arc toward his face. The teacher mentions that this demonstration works about nine times out of ten.

What has the second teacher done differently? This teacher has given the content a dramatic form which has visual impact and is memorable. What did the teacher need to do to conceive this demonstration?

1. The teacher needed to analyze his audience. What did they need in order for him to get their attention from other competitive stimuli?

2. The teacher needed to figure out how the content was pertinent to dramatic frame. A dramatic frame just for the sake of a dramatic frame is a "cheat."

3. The teacher needed to have the minimal skills—physical, organizational, and interpersonal—to execute the dramatic frame.

The way the second teacher handled the content represents a more effective style than the first. The second teacher analyzed and executed the content better and actively worked to present it. The second teacher thought about the complex problem of teaching interactively and attempted to resolve it.

Style as Consistently Recurring Association

If the physics teacher periodically used dramatic frames to teach, a pattern of association would be established in the way he or she presents content. This consistently recurring association of behaviors is the teacher's style of communicating; it is very powerful because it has the capacity to create experiences. The expectations in themselves are form-giving. That is, if a student expects the teacher to be dramatic, cognitive sets are triggered; there may be enhanced attentiveness and readiness to enjoy the presentation. Simultaneously, pressure is put on the teacher to frame materials in such a way that the content is memorable.

Because recurring associations are continually established for each person in repeated encounters with another, it is impossible not to have style. People associate patterns of interaction; to the extent that the patterns of association are salient, they give form to expectations. Consequently, "the *way* a person communicates to a large extent determines self-identity and affects others' perceptions of the individual" (Norton, 1983, p. 19). To the extent that the patterns of association are consistent, the expectations are perceived as reliable.

Every communicative interaction contributes to determining a style profile. As such, norms are constantly shaped, usually reinforced, and ever present as implicit criteria. Hence, a deviation in light of an established norm adds intensity to the form-giving function of style. The absence of an established norm violates expectations and, in the process, sets the stage for a message out of the ordinary. In short, most style profiles are variable, but sufficiently patterned to create resistant expectations (Norton, 1983, p. 50).

A teacher manifests many, sometimes overlapping, facets of style. Being dramatic and entertaining are the more visible facets, but there are an infinite number of other ways to frame content. In my earlier research on communicator style, eleven dimensions of style were identified. For each dimension, several teacher self-descriptions are provided. These are described in Table 2.

Consider the construct of dramatic style. There are many ways to manifest a dramatic style. One teacher may be very witty, while another tells many anecdotes, and still another uses physical humor. The dramatic communicator vividly, emotionally, or strikingly signals that literal meaning is being emphasized to manipulate mood, change energy, or seek attention. With this construct, the form-giving function is emphasis. The intended response is change of some kind—moods are transformed or shifted, energy is increased or decreased, attention is focused or refocused. It does not matter whether the person is being perceived as dramatic because he is gossiping, insulting, telling stories, acting out scenarios, joking, or pantomiming. Each manifestation emphasizes!

Pragmatic Criteria

One of the pragmatic implications of research into style work is to ask at what level individuals make associations. At one of the lowest levels of style, a researcher might focus on the micro-momentary behaviors of the teacher, charting every gesture, facial twitch, and slumped posture. However, this level of analysis makes little sense. Individuals process larger chunks of information. If a person asks what a teacher's style of communication is, the answer is rarely phrased in terms of micro-momentary behaviors: "Joe's style of communication? Well, he has a lot of eyebrow raises, frequent dampened smiles, and infrequent pupil dilation." Rather, the answer is expressed in larger units of analysis: "Joe's style of communication? Well, he is a very energetic teacher who is not only humorous, but also precise."

In light of this, reconsider the dramatic style construct. At the pragmatic level, interventions to improve the effectiveness of a teacher by emphasizing the importance of a dramatic style would take some of the following forms:

Table 2. Items from the Communication Style Measure (Short Form)

Impression-Leaving

What I say usually leaves an impression on people.
I leave people with an impression of me which they definitely tend to remember.
The way I say something usually leaves an impression on people.
I leave a definite impression on people.

Contentious

When I disagree with somebody I am very quick to challenge them.
Once I get wound up in a heated discussion, I have a hard time stopping myself.
It bothers me to drop an argument that is not resolved.
I am very argumentative.

Open

As a rule, I openly express my feelings and emotions.
I readily reveal personal things about myself.
Usually I tell people a lot about myself even if I do not know them well.
I am an extremely open communicator.

Dramatic

Regularly I tell jokes, anecdotes, and stories when I communicate.
Often I physically and vocally act out what I want to communicate.
I very frequently use verbal exaggeration to emphasize a point.
I dramatize a lot.

Dominant

In most social situations I tend to come on strong.
In most social situations I speak very frequently.
I try to take charge of things when I am with people.
I am dominant in social situations.

Precise

Very often I insist that other people document or present some kind of proof for
what they are arguing.
I like to be strictly accurate when I communicate.
In arguments I insist upon very precise definitions.
I am a very precise communicator.

Relaxed

I do not have nervous mannerisms in my speech.
Under pressure I come across as a relaxed speaker.
The rhythm or flow of my speech is not affected by nervousness.
I am a very relaxed communicator.

Friendly

I readily express admiration for others.
To be friendly, I habitually acknowledge verbally other's contributions.
Whenever I communicate, I tend to be very encouraging to people.
I am always an extremely friendly communicator.

Attentive

I really like to listen very carefully to people.
I can always repeat back to a person exactly what was meant.
Usually, I deliberately react in such a way that people know that I am listening to
them.
I am an extremely attentive communicator.

Animated

My eyes reflect exactly what I am feeling when I communicate.
I tend to constantly gesture when I communicate.
I actively use a lot of facial expressions when I communicate.
I am very expressive nonverbally in social situations.

Table 2. (Short Form) *(continued)*

Communicator image

I am a very good communicator.

I always find it very easy to communicate on a one-to-one basis with strangers.

In a small group of strangers I am a very good communicator.

I find it extremely easy to maintain a conversation with a member of the opposite sex whom I have just met.

---

1. Anticipate how to catch attention. Communicative behaviors to do this include use of humor, curiosity, suspense, emotion, analogy, metaphors, surprise, and narratives. The good teacher uses attention-getting forms to emphasize content.

2. Use more energy when teaching. Good teaching requires work at three points: preparation, presentation, and critique. The preparation includes not only organizing notes, but also anticipating how the notes will be presented. The presentational phase entails the most obvious expenditure of energy. Very often it involves being more dynamic, active, open, mentally alert, enthusiastic, and forceful. It frequently requires employing more vocal variety (emphasis, intonation, volume variation) and nonverbal variety to increase expressiveness. The critique phase includes examining what went well and poorly, and then figuring out ways to improve.

3. Learn how to make the class laugh. This is not to say that the teacher needs to be a comic or a clown. As Jean Civikly explains in Chapter 7 of this volume, learning to make someone laugh requires understanding shared premises and points of tension.

4. Learn what entertains a class. The point is not to become an entertainer, but to learn what it would take to entertain the class. This skill can easily be adapted to any subject matter. A good chemistry teacher can vividly describe the composition of an element in an entertaining way without resorting to irrelevant conceits.

5. Learn how to manipulate the mood of a class. This entails many complexities, including a strong sense of timing, a quickness in seeing connections to all sorts of class situations and student behaviors, and the confidence to try such maneuvering.

Each of the above can contribute concretely to a dramatic style of communicating, if that is what is needed. Other style components can be identified in like manner and employed by the teacher to enhance learning.

Conclusion

Stylistic frames are not random; they are chosen to have a particular impact. Individuals make stylistic decisions that are motivated and that are used to motivate. Each of us intentionally frames the content at some level. Some choices work better than others in establishing interactive thought and behavior.

40

The receiver of a message must process both the content and the style messages. The literal content only makes sense in light of how the content was communicated. It is impossible for the student not to process style elements. It is obvious to a student when a teacher uses such "lazy frames" for content as reading from the text or notes, or when a teacher depends only on such frames as "It'll be on the test." On the other hand, it is just as apparent to a student when a teacher uses frames that do extra communicative work.

The extraordinary teachers among us make better motivated distinctions in getting the content across to the students. An appropriately framed message motivates; it is memorable; it enhances learning.

References

Axelrod, J. "From Counterculture to Counterrevolution: A Teacher Career, 1959–1984." In K. E. Eble (Ed.), *Improving Teaching Styles.* New Directions for Teaching and Learning, no. 1. San Francisco: Jossey-Bass, 1980.

Eble, K. E. *The Craft of Teaching: A Guide to Mastering the Professor's Art.* San Francisco: Jossey-Bass, 1976.

Eble, K. E. "Teaching Styles and Faculty Behaviors." In K. E. Eble (Ed.), *Improving Teaching Styles.* New Directions for Teaching and Learning, no. 1. San Francisco: Jossey-Bass, 1980.

Norton, R. W. *Communicator Style: Theory, Applications, and Measures.* Beverly Hills, Calif.: Sage, 1983.

Wiggins, J. *Personality and Prediction: Principles of Personality Assessment.* Reading, Mass.: Addison-Wesley, 1973.

Robert W. Norton is professor of Communication at Purdue University in West Lafayette, Indiana.

*Nonverbal behavior, a communication process poorly
understood and controlled by most teachers, can
greatly enhance the image of the teacher and the
affective learning of students.*

Instructor Nonverbal Communication: Listening to Our Silent Messages

Janis F. Andersen

Successful instruction, learning, and communication are inextricably linked. Both communication and instruction are processes that attempt to establish meaning, transmit messages and influence thinking. Both are said to occur when information is exchanged or behavior is altered. The communication process is the primary means by which instruction is accomplished, contributing substantially to student learning. This chapter examines one aspect of the relationship between communication and instruction by emphasizing instructors' nonverbal behaviors that enhance student learning.

Obviously, college instruction can be improved in a variety of ways. Better facilities, better students, better instructional materials, and better teachers improve instruction. In fact, many of these components interact with each other. For example, excellent materials encourage better instruction from teachers which creates greater student motivation. However, in an era of tighter budgets and declining or steady-state financial support for instructional facilities and materials, instructor improvement is a most important resource. Most instructors recognize that teaching becomes more rewarding as one becomes more effective, and most want to improve their teaching.

J. M. Civikly, (Ed.). *Communicating in College Classrooms.*
New Directions for Teaching and Learning, no. 26. San Francisco: Jossey-Bass, June 1986.

An important factor in the communication process, contributing substantially to instructional effectiveness, is the instuctor's nonverbal behavior. Yet this is not well understood or widely recognized as an instructional asset. There are at least four explanations for this oversight. First, the bulk of research in the area has been conducted in the past decade and has not been disseminated widely in readily available sources. (See Wulff, 1983, for a selected bibliography.) Second, this research consists of isolated studies from a variety of disciplines which were not integrated conceptually until recently. Woolfolk and Brooks (1983) offer a helpful integrative review of the influence of nonverbal communication in teaching. Third, the importance of nonverbal behavior in the instructional process has been acknowledged in elementary and secondary settings but largely ignored for college classrooms (Smith, 1979). Perhaps this results from an assumption that college students learn what they need to regardless of teaching competence, or from a university norm that teaching is secondary to research and university service. Our educational system mirrors this value by requiring elementary and secondary teachers to study teaching while assuming that college professors automatically have adequate teaching skills. Content competence and instructional competence are presumed to be one and the same capability.

Finally, nonverbal communication may not have received educators' serious attention because of popularization and trivialization of the area. Beginning with Julius Fast's bestseller *Body Language,* and continuing with numerous popular magazine articles and television news specials, the American public has become aware of the influence of nonverbal communication. Many of those sources, however, have depicted this body of knowledge as a new weapon for superficial, self-serving, manipulative, and upwardly mobile individuals. Publicized claims were overly simple, frequently inaccurate, and often more akin to astrology than to science. With this shadow obscuring the significance of the area, it is not surprising that many serious scholars and readers have largely ignored the literature of nonverbal communication. For whatever reasons, few college professors are aware of how to use their nonverbal behavior to enhance instructional effectiveness.

Definition of Terms

Although communication scholars differ on definitions of "communication" and "nonverbal behavior," statements of these terms are necessary if we are to share a common referent. *Communication* is a process that occurs whenever one person stimulates meaning in the mind of a receiver or changes the behavior of a receiver. It is not necessarily an intentional process, nor is it always a conscious one. Communication and behavior are inseparable; any behavior has communicative potential that is realized when meaning is attached to the behavior by a receiver. *Nonverbal* refers to communicative messages which are nonlinguistic, analogic, and processed primarily by the brain's right hemisphere (Andersen and others, 1979b). Gestures, facial expressions, physical appearance, touching behavior, spatial arrangement, and paralanguage are generally nonverbal messages. However, sign language is most commonly classified as verbal communication even though it uses gestures, since it is linguistic, often digital (particularly when finger spelling), and usually processed in the brain's left or language hemisphere. A few messages are difficult to classify as verbal or nonverbal. Understanding of the area is facilitated if nonverbal and verbal are thought of as two ends of a message continuum: Some messages may be classified as more verbal or more nonverbal in nature.

In classroom settings, verbal and nonverbal messages occur together—reinforcing, undercutting, emphasizing, regulating, modifying, accenting, complementing, and contradicting each other. While this chapter focuses on nonverbal communication by teachers, student nonverbal behavior is equally important and should be considered when attempting to explain or control overall classroom atmosphere. No matter what the source, nonverbal messages are continuous; in the presence of another person, it is impossible not to communicate a nonverbal message. Even an attempt to terminate communication by silently staring or leaving a room signals a message. Thus, whether talking or not, instructors are continuously communicating. Their gestures, body movements, facial expressions, eye behavior, use of space and time, physical appearance, and physique continue to send messages even when they are silent. When talking, their vocal pitch, speaking rate, volume, and accent provide additional nonverbal information.

Influence of Nonverbal Communication

The influence of nonverbal messages on human interaction is substantial. The most widely quoted statistic (Mehrabian, 1972) claims that 93 percent of the meaning in human interaction comes from nonverbal messages, while only 7 percent emanates from verbal messages. Although many researchers do not support such a large estimate, the significance of nonverbal communication in interactions is not questioned. Two studies that directly measured the relative importance of nonverbal communication in an instructional setting found it to be more important than the verbal component (Balzer, 1969; Keith and others, 1974).

In classroom settings, teacher and student communication behaviors influence each other. Communication is largely a reciprocal act—we give people what we perceive they have given us. The origination of reciprocity is difficult to isolate—it is a chicken-egg argument—but a participant can alter the cycle at any point. Even though the instructor's communication is also influenced by the cycle, he or she is in a good directing position to alter classroom communication.

Functions of Nonverbal Communication

Nonverbal communication behaviors serve many functions: they communicate warmth and affect; indicate approval or disapproval of others; define the nature of the relationship; indicate relative power and status; reveal current emotional states; regulate and pace verbal exchanges; provide cues for impression formation; influence and persuade; reveal one's level of tension or relaxation; indicate one's culture, values, attitudes, gender, and background; and influence the performance of others (Rosenfeld and Civikly, 1976). In instructional settings, nonverbal communication also functions to enhance learning, particularly affective learning.

Communication messages have both content and relational components (Watzlawick and others, 1967). The *content* component is the literal meaning or the denotative verbal translation of the message. The *relationship* component of a message signals the nature of the relationship and suggests how that literal verbal meaning is to be interpreted. For example, the statement "This material is quite difficult but with some effort you will be able to manage" is accompanied by very different meanings depending on the relationship of the interactants. When said by one student to another it could be a compliment or an insult. The sincerity of the difficulty claim, the relationship between the students, and the speaker's degree of familiarity with the receiver's ability create differing interpretations of the message's content. If the instructor makes this statement to a student, it might be a challenge, an accurate assessment of difficulty and ability, or a belittling insult. It could suggest that the student recognizes the instructor's power, or it could signal the instructor's concern. The relational components of messages often alter the meaning of the message in subtle and confusing ways. Nonverbal communication functions as a device to signal how the content or literal component of the message is to be interpreted and understood.

Nonverbal Communication and Learning

Nonverbal communication has its most direct instructional impact on the affective domain of learning, which is concerned with student likes and dislikes, attitudes, values, beliefs, appreciations, and interests. In addition to learning facts and concepts, students also learn attitudes towards the content area and predispositional patterns that motivate them to use that knowledge in their lives. The affective domain centers on these learned attitudes and orientations toward the subject area (Krathwohl and others, 1964).

Although college instructors seldom address this domain directly, affective learning is a valued goal. No matter what discipline we teach, we share the goal of creating lifelong learners. For example, English instructors hope students retain their ability to analyze a play or a novel but also hope to motivate them to attend plays and read novels after they complete the literature class. Few music instructors would claim success if their students learned to recognize the works of classical composers but developed an aversion to classical music in the process. Students who learn the laws of physics or biology in the classroom but never think about them after the semester ends have not been well educated. In any discipline, we are interested not only in cognitive or psychomotor learning, but also in creating positive student affect towards the content area.

The instructor's communicative behavior in general and nonverbal behavior in particular has a significant impact on affective learning. In one study (Andersen, 1979), almost one-fourth of the variation in both student liking for the content area and student desires to take future courses in the content area was a function of the instructor's nonverbal behavior. Over half of the variation in student liking for the instructor was the result of the instructor's nonverbal communication. These nonverbal messages of liking and affect require further discussion.

Nonverbal Liking and Affect. The communication of liking or positive affect is largely a nonverbal phenomenon. Instructors seldom verbalize their feelings, yet students seem to know instructors' attitudes toward students, content areas, and the general teaching process. Students infer these affective data from the instructor's nonverbal behaviors.

Factor-analytic studies indicate that positive affect is communicated through a cluster of nonverbal behaviors, labeled *immediacy behaviors* (Andersen, 1979; Andersen and others, 1979a). Immediacy behaviors increase arousal and sensory closeness, and communicate social accessibility. The nonverbal behaviors most closely associated with the immediacy cluster include eye contact, smiling, vocal expressiveness, physical proximity, appropriate touching, leaning toward a person, gesturing, using overall body movements, being relaxed, and spending time with someone. Andersen and Andersen (1982) provide a detailed review of nonverbal immediacy as it functions in instruction.

In short, immediacy behaviors communicate feelings of warmth and support and engender feelings of interpersonal attraction. Individuals behave in immediate ways when involved with others they like, and they like others who also behave in immediate ways. Immediacy is a spontaneous manifestation of positive affect and is processed, often unconsciously, as such. In classroom settings, instructors who use nonverbal immediacy behaviors manifest greater liking and affect towards their students and engender higher student affect. The climate of positive affect extends beyond the interactants to the subject matter and the discipline (Andersen and Andersen, 1982).

It is important to realize that immediacy behaviors, like most non-verbal impressions, are processed as a gestalt or holistic impression. Therefore, instructors wishing to increase immediacy should select those immediacy behaviors with which they feel most comfortable. If an instructor is perceived as cold, distant, or aloof, he or she can consciously engage in additional immediacy to enhance perceptions of warmth and increase affective learning. However, instructors who feel cold, negative, and aloof towards students because they dislike teaching or dislike "those immature undergraduates" will probably have trouble feigning immediacy. Considerable nonverbal research indicates that true feelings leak to receivers in a number of ways (Mehrabian, 1971). Thus, a sincere positive attitude is a crucial prerequisite for the successful communication of immediacy. Interestingly, some research (Collins, 1976) indicates that teachers trained to be more immediate and enthusiastic do begin to feel more positive towards teaching.

An additional manifestation of high affect occurs when persons mirror each other's body positions and synchronize with each other's behaviors. Interactants who like each other match each other's body orientations, speech and pause rates, gestures, eye behavior, and posture. Mirroring is difficult to do consciously, although some counselors suggest this as an effective strategy to increase client trust and satisfaction, yet it seems to occur without effort once the positive affect develops. This may explain why instructors who generate high student affect seldom have discipline or classroom control problems. The entire class group is "in synch" and is coordinated with the instructor.

Regulation of Talk. One of the major functions of nonverbal communication is to regulate verbal interaction. Individuals use nonverbal messages to indicate when they wish to speak and when they wish to give the speaking turn to another person. Through eye contact, they even designate who will be the next speaker. Nonverbally, instructors signal that it is a student's turn to talk by dropping their pitch, dropping gestures, relaxing and leaning back slightly, and ending a vocal phrase by looking directly at the student expected to respond. An instructor can shorten student responses and acquire the speaking floor more quickly by nodding his or her head rapidly, opening his or her mouth as if to talk, inhaling, gesturing, leaning forward, and verbalizing during the first pause that is accompanied by eye contact.

These subtle cues provide a smooth conversational flow, making interruptions the rude exception rather than the norm. In classrooms, turn-taking is formalized somewhat with hand raising, but the same regulating cues play an important role. If a teacher wishes to curtail an overly eager student's contributions, this can be done tactfully. Rather than ignore, avoid, or embarrass the student into speaking less, the instructor can acknowledge him or her through eye contact that occurs while the instructor is in the middle of an utterance. This timing of eye contact will signal recognition but will not invite verbal reaction. At the end of the utterance, the instructor should avoid eye contact with the overly eager student and consciously look directly at another student. Unless that student is extremely reticent, he or she will feel the conversational pressure and provide a response.

Classroom Control. In addition to regulating conversations, nonverbal behavior allows teachers to implement control strategies that are more agreeable to students. Few individuals like to be scolded or ridiculed, and many resent authoritarian attempts to control. Skilled leaders use nonverbal behavior to subtly direct others' behaviors. Instructors can, for example, use eye contact, facial expressions, and simple gestures to regulate unwanted interaction, stimulate desired behavior, and remind students of the teacher's position.

Unwanted extraneous interaction can also be curtailed tactfully through nonverbal communication. For example, students who disrupt class attention by their side talking often believe that they are doing it unnoticed. Consider how seldom such disruption occurs from students seated in the front-center of the room. The instructor can decrease this unwanted interaction by simply making the students aware of the instructor's presence through increased eye contact or movement that places the ambling lecturer near the conversing students. This control may cause the talkers to feel a bit embarrassed or apologetic, but tends to eliminate the defensive me-against-you climate that often occurs when they are chided in public.

From my workshop experiences with instructors, I have found that stimulating desired student interaction is an important goal. This goal is largely accomplished through nonverbal behavior. Ironically, instructors who express a desire for more student interaction may fail to give their students nonverbal signals of this goal. Instructor immediacy behaviors such as smiling, gesturing, being vocally expressive, and reducing spatial barriers create greater student rapport and improve the likelihood of interaction. Use of nonverbal conversational regulators that give the floor to students also heightens class interaction. Instructors often fail to establish eye contact with students, stay poised as if to continue speaking, hold their gestures and their pitch, and pause only for a brief moment. These nonverbal cues signal that the verbal attempt to stimulate interaction should be interpreted as a rhetorical question rather than as a true invitation to participate.

One of the most effective means for stimulating interaction is pause time accompanied by direct eye contact. When teachers do this, students feel the conversational pressure. However, the pause time may need to be ten to fifteen seconds—an awkward silence for most students and instructors. Learning to feel comfortable with this pause time is an important step in generating greater student participation.

48

Finally, a supportive and productive classroom climate can be enhanced through the instructor's nonverbal messages of power and status. The literature on attraction suggests that we like those who are of high status and power and who are in a position to reward us (Berscheid and Walster, 1978). Yet we dislike persons who verbally proclaim their worth and power. Nonverbal communication can be a non-offensive means of reminding others of power and status. Behaviors associated with dominance, power, and status include eye contact (even staring), relaxed but not slumped posture, expressive and expansive gestures, touch initiation, classic clothing and personal artifacts, expansive use of space, and poised, straightforward posture. New instructors, teaching assistants, and others less confident or experienced in their teaching, tend to behave in nonverbally submissive ways. Since many women are often socialized to be nonverbally submissive, they may profit from assertive nonverbal styles. Assertive behaviors signal the instructor's importance and credibility; students tend to respond appropriately. Thus, instructors perceived to have high power and status have less need for classroom control and are free to interact with students without fear of losing control and respect.

Conclusion

Nonverbal communication is largely responsible for establishing relationships among persons in the classroom and elsewhere. This chapter describes how nonverbal behavior by instructors can directly alter teacher image and have an impact on student affect and learning. Through nonverbal messages, individuals signal how they feel towards each other. Instructors who generate high student affect not only improve their self-esteem, feel liked by their students, and receive higher student evaluations; they also generate more affective learning for the subject matter and their academic discipline. In the short run, higher affective learning enhances the popularity of the subject matter and increases student enrollments. In the long run, higher affect is the avenue to lifelong learning, more general support for education, and a better society. Thus, whether for pragmatic reasons such as increased student enrollments and increased funding, or for philosophical goals such as a better-educated society, the mechanisms that generate high student affect should remain a central concern. Nonverbal communication by instructors is a primary method of generating and sustaining student affect.

References

Andersen, J. F. "The Relationship Between Teacher Immediacy and Teaching Effectiveness." In D. Nimmo (Ed.), *Communication Yearbook 3*. New Brunswick, N.J.: Transaction Books, 1979.

Andersen, J. F., Andersen, P. A., and Jensen, A. D. "The Measurement of Nonverbal Immediacy." *Journal of Applied Communication Research*, 1979a, 7, 153-180.

Andersen, P. A., Garrison, J. P., and Andersen, J. F. "Implication of a Neurophysiological Approach for the Study of Nonverbal Communication." *Human Communication Research*, 1979b, 6 (1), 74-89.

Andersen, P. A., and Andersen, J. F. "Nonverbal Immediacy in Instruction." In L. L. Barker (Ed..), *Communication in the Classroom*. Englewood Cliffs, N.J.: Prentice-Hall, 1982.

Balzer, L. "Nonverbal and Verbal Behaviors of Biology Teachers." *American Biology Teacher*, 1969, 31, 226-229.

Berscheid, E., and Walster, E. H. *Interpersonal Attraction*. (2nd ed.) Reading, Mass.: Addison-Wesley, 1978.

Collins, M. L. *The Effects of Training for Enthusiasm on the Enthusiasm Displayed by Preservice Elementary Teachers*, 1976. (ED 130-337)

Keith, L. T., Tornatzky, L. G., and Pettigrew, L. E. "An Analysis of Verbal and Nonverbal Classroom Teaching Behaviors." *Journal of Experimental Education*, 1974, 42 (4), 30-38.

Krathwohl, D. R., Bloom, B. S., and Masia, B. *A Taxonomy of Educational Objectives, Handbook II: The Affective Domain*. New York: David McKay, 1964.

Mehrabian, A. *Silent Messages*. Belmont, Calif.: Wadsworth, 1971.

Mehrabian, A. *Nonverbal Communication*. Chicago: Aldine-Asherton, 1972.

Rosenfeld, L. B., and Civikly, J. M. *With Words Unspoken: The Nonverbal Experience*. New York: Holt, Rinehart and Winston, 1976.

Smith, H. A. "Nonverbal Communication in Teaching." *Review of Educational Research*, 1979, 49 (4), 631-672.

Watzlawick, P., Beavin, J. H., and Jackson, D. D. *Pragmatics of Human Communication*. New York: Norton, 1967.

Woolfolk, A. E., and Brooks, D. M. "Nonverbal Communication in Teaching." *Review of Research in Education*, 1983, 10, 103-149.

Wulff, D. "Selected Bibliography: Nonverbal Communication in the Educational Context." *The Communicator*, 1983, 13, 23-36.

Janis F. Andersen is associate professor of Speech Communication at San Diego State University. She has served as chair of the instructional development divisions of the Speech Communication Association and the International Communication Association.

Teaching involves a process of relational development.
Its effectiveness depends on application of relevant
interpersonal competencies.

Teaching as Relational Development

Joseph A. DeVito

Given the current trend toward larger classes, multimedia instruction, and the use of computers as surrogate teachers, it may seem paradoxical to point out that teaching is a relational process and to suggest that superior teaching depends on the development of effective interpersonal communication skills. Whatever the subject matter or instructional method, establishing an interpersonal relationship with students is both feasible and necessary.

Relational Development

Theory and research on interpersonal relationships are sufficiently well established to offer assistance to any teacher. *Relational development* refers to the processes involved in creating an interpersonal relationship, from first contact through intimacy and possibly to dissolution. Social psychological models, first proposed by Altman and Taylor (1973) and Levinger (1977), identified the variables that influence stages of relationship development, maintenance, and deterioration. Models having a communication perspective, such as those offered by Krug (1982), Knapp (1984), and DeVito (1986), serve primarily to describe the communication messages that are exchanged throughout an interpersonal relationship. The major stages in each of these models appear in Table 1.

J. M. Civikly, (Ed.). *Communicating in College Classrooms.*
New Directions for Teaching and Learning, no. 26. San Francisco: Jossey-Bass, June 1986.

Table 1. Models of Relational Development

Altman and Taylor (1973)	Levinger (1977)	Krug (1982)	Knapp (1984)	DeVito (1986)
Orientation	Zero Contact Awareness Surface Contact	Initiation	Initiating	Contact
Exploratory Affective Exchange	Mutuality Moderate Intersection	Experimentation Liking Trial	Experimenting Intensifying	Involvement
Affective Exchange Stable Exchange	Major Intersection	Coupling Stabilization-Nurturance	Integrating Bonding	Intimacy
		Stabilization-Conflict Devel-opment	Differentiating Circumscribing Stagnating Avoiding	Deterioration
		Termination Avoidance Maintenance	Terminating	Dissolution

It is useful not only to view teaching as an interpersonal process, but also to explore how teaching follows the life cycle of a personal relationship. By using this approach, we can articulate more clearly the requisite teacher skills and competencies. While some of these skills are traditional to teacher preparation programs, others are new and demand a different perception of the teacher's role.

The intent of this chapter is not to imply that a good teacher-student relationship is the sole goal of teaching. Rather, the development of the interpersonal relationship is viewed as the means by which more effective, efficient, and satisfying teaching and learning may take place. This, it seems, is what Gilbert Highet intended when he observed that one of the essentials of good teaching is "to like the pupils" (1950, p. 25). If a teacher does not like pupils, Highet advises that person to "give up teaching."

Assumptions Concerning Teaching and Relational Development

At the outset to this life-cycle perspective, four basic assumptions need statement.

Assumption 1. Teaching can be described as a relational process from initial contact, through intimacy, to dissolution. As seen in Table 1, the stages between initial contact and dissolution have varying degrees of specificity. Typically, teachers and students experience the stages of experimentation, norm-testing, stabilization, stagnation, and dissolution.

Assumption 2. Teaching can be best understood, described, and improved by treating it as a relational development process. The reasoning here is simple: Teacher-student interaction that assists teaching and learning depends in great part on the development of an interpersonal relationship.

Assumption 3. The development of an interpersonal relationship between teacher and student will lead to more effective learning and greater satisfaction for both student and teacher. Relevant here is research indicating that interpersonal interactions are more influential in changing attitudes and behaviors than are the various media (DeVito, 1985). This finding may reflect the preference of students and teachers for instruction by human beings rather than by media alone.

Assumption 4. When teaching fails, that failure (or some significant part thereof) can be attributed to the ineffectiveness of the relational development process. When we view the teaching process as relational development, we assert a preference for dialogue rather than the traditional monologue. This preference implies that the teacher and student are co-contributors: Both are listeners; both are speakers. Both care for, respect, and support each other. Both are learners and both are teachers. It is a view of communication in which I-Thou (as opposed to I-It) relationships are cultivated and nourished (Buber, 1958; Thomlison, 1982).

Finally, teaching as relational development implies that there are now three selves, three "personalities" that must be identified, addressed, and nourished: (1) the student, (2) the teacher, and (3) the student-teacher relationship. This view, modified from James and Savary's (1976) conception of friendship, demands that attention be directed to all three identities. Effective teaching, like effective relationships, cannot be developed or maintained without direct and concerted attention to the third self, the teacher-student relationship.

Relational Stages

Drawing on the various relational models, a seven-stage educational process model is proposed.

Stage 1: Precontact. At the precontact stage, we identify the teacher's and students' preconceptions, attitudinal predispositions, belief structures, predictions and prophecies, prior successes or failures, competencies, interests, and other factors that may influence the relationship. Positive expectations, a history of classroom success, superior levels of competence, and strong interest in the subject matter will influence the student-teacher relationship in ways drastically different from negative expectations, a history of classroom failure, and so forth.

Stage 2: Awareness. In Levinger's model (1977), awareness is divided into two types: unilateral and bilateral. This distinction is particularly relevant to initial contact between student and teacher. The student-teacher relationship clearly begins with unilateral awareness, the awareness the student has of the teacher but which the teacher does not have of the student. Only through interaction will the awareness become bilateral, though perhaps never totally equal.

Stage 3: Contact. At the contact stage, student and teacher communicate, nonverbally at first, and then verbally. Personal appearance, facial expression, vocal tone, and manner of speaking operate simultaneously for both the students and the teacher.

These first impressions possess a number of characteristics relevant to the teaching-learning process. First, the impressions are inevitable and form despite attempts to avoid prejudging anyone. Second, they have a powerful effect on how the relationship progresses. Third, and perhaps most important, these impressions are resistant to change. The primacy effect (the tendency to give disproportionate weight to what is perceived first) operates like a filter through which later impressions pass. Confirmatory information, we know, is received more easily and retained longer than contradictory information. First impressions, then, are crucial for the student, the teacher, and the teacher-student relationship.

Stage 4: Involvement. At the involvement stage, there is a testing of each other, a testing of personalities and relational dispositions. When we learn about individuals in the class, we begin to see each other as unique, as distinct from the stereotyped "teacher" and "student" role positions held initially. Regrettably, accounts from students and teachers suggest that many classes never reach this stage of involvement.

Stage 5: Intimacy. In a teacher-student relationship, intimacy involves a significant expansion in breadth and depth—we begin to talk about more issues and penetrate more deeply into our individual value structures and personalities (Altman and Taylor, 1973). We emphasize perceptions of each other as individuals rather than as roles, responding to each other as unique entities. At this stage we are able not only to predict another's behavior but to explain it as well. And perhaps most important is that we operate with our own system of rules rather than the culture's. Communication rules that are distinctive to the persons comprising the class reflect this unique situation (Miller and Steinberg, 1975).

Stage 6: Deterioration. In romantic relationships, deterioration is usually viewed as problematic and negative. It is the time when bonds between persons are loosened. In the teaching situation, this stage has a more positive tone. It represents a normal and healthy developmental process in which the student is preparing to separate from the mentor, not unlike the bird leaving its nest.

Stage 7: Dissolution. The final stage represents the physical separation of student and teacher. Dissolution makes it possible for each to formulate new relationships that hold possibilities for new learning.

Relationship Skills for Teachers

Given this conception of the teaching-learning process, a number of relational skills become important for the teacher.

1. *The ability to communicate effectively in interpersonal interactions.* Though the traditional skills of public speaking are not irrelevant, the interpersonal skills are emphasized here. These skills may be defined in terms of both humanistic qualities (empathy, openness, supportiveness, equality, and positiveness) and pragmatic qualities (other-orientation, interaction management, expressiveness, immediacy, and confidence) (DeVito, 1986; Spitzberg and Cupach, 1984).

2. *The ability to initiate and encourage meaningful dialogue that progresses from surface to deeper levels.* This dialogue is essential not only between teacher and student, but also among students. It is a skill that students as well as teachers must develop. In so doing, it is helpful for the teacher to express the importance of such dialogue and to serve as a model.

3. *The ability to control degrees of openness and self-disclosure.* According to Sidney Jourard (1971), the ability to reveal oneself to others

and to be open and receptive to others' self-revelations is central to one's psychological well-being and to the ultimate goal of self-knowledge. Jourard holds that one can only know oneself by sharing that self with others. He identifies two guidelines for approaching self-knowledge. First, be open with others about the qualities that make you unique, such as opinions, feelings, hopes, and disappointments. Second, seek feedback from others about yourself to determine how effectively and accurately you are being perceived. The potential rewards and risks of such openness must be assessed for specific situations. Nevertheless, the ability to express personal information when appropriate is a primary skill in the relational development view of teaching.

Such sharing of self is an interpersonal process—there must be a sender and a receiver. Accordingly, in responding to another's openness, one should demonstrate the skills of effective listening, express support for the person (while avoiding evaluation), keep the disclosures confidential, and avoid using the disclosed information against the person in any way.

Research on gender differences in self-disclosure suggests that women, who are traditionally more concerned with relational issues, are more likely to share information about themselves than are men. Women who choose to avoid such openness attribute this to their fear of damaging the relationship. Men, on the other hand, explain their reluctance to be open as a fear of losing control of the situation (Rosenfeld, 1979). These findings lend support to the proposed relational development model that emphasizes the interpersonal dynamics of teaching. Further support is found in the observations of Eble: "In a dozen years of speaking to hundreds of faculty groups assembled to discuss teaching, I have been struck by the fact that women faculty attend in greater numbers in proportion to their numbers on the faculty than men. Less confidently, I would say that women faculty often show a more intense interest in teaching and a greater responsiveness to its widest dimensions than men. A number of surveys have given evidence that women value teaching as a main source of satisfaction more than men" (1983, p. 52).

4. *The ability to compliment, reinforce, and reward.* Many public school teacher preparation programs include units on ways to punish undesirable behaviors, despite Skinner's (1968) repeated arguments that reward controls behavior more effectively than does punishment. The willingness to reward, and the skills for doing so—such as using positive language (Cooper, 1984) and giving praise and compliments—need to be mastered by the teacher.

5. *The ability to establish, maintain, and relinquish control.* Obviously, control needs to be established by the teacher in a variety of situations, and training programs have taught teachers well in this respect. However, another important skill, that of relinquishing control or handing control over to the student, seems to have been neglected (Douvan, 1977).

6. *The ability to deal effectively with conflict and to utilize conflict strategies that are productive of meaningful dialogue.* Contrary to popular belief, conflict is not always negative. If a class is without conflict, it is probably dealing with insignificant issues. Productive conflict is guided by principles of effective interpersonal communication, such as openness, equality, positiveness, empathy, and supportiveness. The following behaviors can help make conflict productive: (1) state your position directly and honestly; (2) react openly to the students' messages; (3) express ownership of your thoughts and feelings; (4) address the real and present issues that are causing the conflict; (5) describe the behaviors causing the conflict; (6) demonstrate empathic understanding; (7) validate the feelings of the student; (8) express your feelings spontaneously, not strategically; (9) state your position tentatively and provisionally; (10) capitalize on agreements; (11) express positive feelings for the student; (12) avoid ridicule and sarcasm; and (13) involve yourself in the conflict by playing an active role as both sender and receiver (DeVito, 1986). As Joyce Hocker explains in her chapter on teacher-student conflicts, there are two criteria for determining a productive conflict: The *issue* is resolved; and the *relationship* is not damaged but enhanced.

7. *The ability to listen actively and to use what is said to create a meaningful dialogue.* More specific skills might be identified as follows: listen for feelings as well as for thoughts; search for the student's surface and underlying messages; paraphrase the student's meanings; ask questions if necessary to determine the accuracy of meanings; express acceptance of the student's feelings; and encourage the student to explore further his or her feelings and thoughts.

8. *The ability to decipher relational as well as content messages and to develop a sensitivity to the verbal and nonverbal cues through which relational messages are often sent.* Information about the relationship and how the literal message (the content) should be interpreted can be found in such nonverbal carriers as vocal tone, facial expressions, and immediacy behaviors. Janis Andersen's chapter in this volume provides a detailed review of these nonverbal messages.

9. *The ability to repair relationships as needed.* In general, this ability would include the following behaviors: (1) avoid withdrawal and keep the channels of communication open; (2) avoid the sudden decrease in interaction that often signals distrust; (3) increase supportiveness; (4) avoid deception; (5) avoid excessive negative responses; and (6) increase the cherishing behaviors that create an environment conducive to compromise and rebuilding (Duck, 1984; Lederer, 1984).

Benefits of Relational Approach to Teaching

Apart from the obvious benefits to teacher and student already noted, three additional ones are identified here. First, this approach places interpersonal communication at the center of the educational process. Education is a developmental process, dependent upon effective interpersonal communication skills.

Second, the relational approach places an enormous body of research on relationships and relational development at the disposal of the educator. Social exchange theory, attraction, self-disclosure, conflict and conflict resolution, relational develoment, and relational repair are just a few of the topics that have recently generated an impressive body of research directly applicable to the teaching-learning process.

Third, this view provides us with a framework and perspective for identifying the communication qualities of the superior teacher and for evaluating teacher performance—or even readiness and suitability to teach. As a working hypothesis, we might postulate such qualities to be similar to those of the effective relational partner. These qualities then need to be recast in terms of the unique student-teacher relationship.

References

Altman, I., and Taylor, D. *Social Penetration: The Development of Interpersonal Relationships.* New York: Holt, Rinehart and Winston, 1973.

Buber, M. *I and Thou.* (2nd ed.) New York: Scribner's, 1958.

Cooper, P. J. *Speech Communication for the Classroom Teacher.* Dubuque, Iowa: Gorsuch Scarisbrick, 1984.

DeVito, J. A. *Human Communication.* (3rd ed.) New York: Harper and Row, 1985.

DeVito, J. A. *The Interpersonal Communication Book.* (4th ed.) New York: Harper and Row, 1986.

Douvan, E. "Interpersonal Relationships: Some Questions and Observations." In G. Levinger and H. L. Raush (Eds.), *Close Relationships: Perspectives on the Meaning of Intimacy.* Amherst: University of Massachusetts Press, 1977.

Duck, S. (Ed.), *Personal Relationships 5: Repairing Personal Relationships.* London: Academic Press, 1984.

Eble, K. E. *The Aims of College Teaching.* San Francisco: Jossey-Bass, 1983.

Highet, G. *The Art of Teaching.* New York: Random House (Vintage), 1950.

James, M., and Savary, L. *The Heart of Friendship.* New York: Harper and Row, 1976.

Jourard, S. M. *The Transparent Self.* New York: Van Nostrand Reinhold, 1971.

Knapp, M. L. *Interpersonal Communication and Human Relationships.* (2nd ed.) Boston: Allyn and Bacon, 1984.

Krug, L. "Alternative Lifestyle Dyads: An Alternative Relationship Paradigm." *Alternative Communications,* 1982, *4,* 32-52.

Lederer, W. J. *Creating a Good Relationship.* New York: Norton, 1984.

Levinger, G. "The Embrace of Lives: Changing and Unchanging." In G. Levinger and H. L. Raush (Eds.), *Close Relationships: Perspectives on the Meaning of Intimacy.* Amherst: Univ. of Massachusetts Press, 1977.

Miller, G. R., and Steinberg, M. *Between People.* Chicago: Science Research Associates, 1975.

Rosenfeld, L. B. "Self-Disclosure Avoidance: Why Am I Afraid to Tell You Who I Am?" *Communication Monographs,* 1979, *46,* 63-74.

Skinner, B. F. *The Technology of Teaching.* New York: Appleton-Century-Crofts, 1968.

Spitzberg, B. H., and Cupach, W. R. *Interpersonal Communication Competence.* Beverly Hills, Calif.: Sage, 1984.
Thomlison, T. D. *Toward Interpersonal Dialogue.* New York: Longman, 1982.

Joseph A. DeVito is professor of Communication at Hunter College of the City University of New York.

Unless a relational base is developed, the teacher's effort to incorporate humor into instruction may go unrewarded.

Humor and the Enjoyment of College Teaching

Jean M. Civikly

Several summers ago, I made a wise decision to enroll in an Intensive Spanish class. Not only did I learn a measure of conversational Spanish, but I also observed humor being used to help the students learn the "foreign" verbs and phrases. Through his energy and intentness, the instructor communicated his enjoyment and love for teaching. He had polished his teaching skills and use of humor to such a degree that a student's fear of speaking in public in an unfamiliar language was transformed into an attractive challenge—avoidance became approach. The incorporation of humor into the language lessons also benefited the instructor. When Sr. Barela told a funny story, *en español,* he was able to determine the students' understanding of the language—laughter (or moans and boos at the puns and corny jokes) let him know that the class had understood. It was a very tactful teaching style and a most pleasant and safe way to learn.

Review of the research on humor and teaching (Zillman and Bryant, 1983) indicates that the role of humor in teaching and learning is a curious one—complex, confusing, and seldom a laughing matter. In *The Art of Teaching,* Gilbert Highet observed that "one of the most important

J. M. Civikly, (Ed.). *Communicating in College Classrooms.*
New Directions for Teaching and Learning, no. 26. San Francisco: Jossey-Bass, June 1986.

qualities of a good teacher is humor. Many are the purposes it serves. The most obvious one is that it keeps the pupils alive and attentive because they are never quite sure what is coming next. . . . The real purpose of humor in teaching is deeper and more worthy. It is to hook the pupils and the teacher, and to link them through enjoyment. When people laugh together, they become one group of human beings enjoying existence " (1950, p. 16).

Before looking at the prominent research on humor in teaching and learning, it will be helpful to ask some questions about using humor in the classroom. Do you use humor in your teaching? If so, in what ways and how often? Is it planned or unintentional? Why do you incorporate humor in your teaching? To maintain control of the class situation? To distance yourself from the students? To embarrass a feisty student or keep a student in his or her "place"? To help students and yourself to relax? To have a good time? To develop a sense of rapport with the students? Any of these goals might apply. Humor is a multifunctional communication tool that can be both a virtue and a vice, depending on how it is used (Civikly, 1983).

Humor as Communication

As is true of other acts of communication, humor involves many variables: a speaker, an audience, a topic-message, a setting, and feedback. Both sender and audience enter the interaction equipped with their own past experiences, abilities, moods, information, and expectations. Even without consideration to an individual's humor style and motives, it is evident that a sizable degree of sophistication and cognitive complexity is needed to assemble these elements and to express and comprehend humorous messages. Although veiled as a simple daily interaction, humor is actually a complex social-psychological communication event.

More important, humor as an act of communication necessarily involves persons and the relationship that exists among those persons. Recent research on student reactions to teacher-initiated humor (Darling and Civikly, 1984) indicated that the development of a relationship between teacher and student is critical to the student's accurate interpretation of teacher humor. Without some relational base, students are unsure of the teacher's motives. This uncertainty, combined with the subordinate position of a "student" who is also being subjected to evaluation and grading by the teacher, can make for a volatile and defensive situation (Rosenfeld, 1983; Darling and Civikly, 1984).

From where does this relational base evolve? "From the teacher-student relationship" is too glib an answer. A relational base involves mutual understanding between teacher and students—some knowledge of the persons in the class and their personalities, attitudes, and styles of interaction. More precise questions should help to clarify this concept. For *teachers*, these questions include the following: What is the composition of the student group (age, gender, cultural-ethnic identifications, marital status, and so forth)? What are the students' expectations for the course and for their participation in the course? What student personal-social needs are evident (for example, needs for positive regard, security, and feelings of inclusion in the class group)? For *students*, the questions might include the following: What teacher characteristics are presented in class (age, gender, cultural-ethnic identification, marital status, personal style, nonverbal presentation, and so forth)? What is the teacher's attitude toward the course, the students, and student participation? What is the teacher's preference for teaching style and enjoyment of teaching the course? What teacher needs exist—need for control, approval, inclusion, or credibility?

Relational bases may form along a number of dimensions: formal to informal, equal to unequal, positive to negative, uncertain to certain/safe. Humor research concludes that laughter and enjoyment are by and large interpersonal events characterized by two feelings: that the relational base is positive, and that it is secure and safe (Ziv, 1984).

Evoking Humorous Responses from Students

Based on the prerequisite for a relational base, if a teacher wishes to encourage use of humor in a class, it is important for that teacher to understand the conditions that evoke humor in the general population. Research has offered a number of theories, no one of which can claim complete explanation of why people laugh. The kingdom of humor obeys a variety of masters.

1. *Incongruity.* People may laugh when two incongrous or unexpected forces are juxtaposed. This concept of "bi-sociation" (Koestler, 1964) is evident, for example, upon hearing a large-bodied man speak in a high-pitched or "female" voice.

2. *Mastery.* People may laugh at what they can master or accomplish, for example, "getting" a joke or solving a puzzle or experiment. The laughter or enjoyment comes from conquering the challenge that is posed.

3. *Psychoanalysis.* People may laugh and use humor to release feelings of aggression, sexual interest, taboo thoughts, or general uneasiness (Freud, [1905] 1960).

4. *Disparagement.* People may laugh at their own foibles and frailties, including self-critical comments.

5. *Superiority.* People may laugh at the misfortune of others and at their own comparative superiority; this may include sexist and ethnic humor, sick jokes, and putdown humor.

6. *Relief-release.* People may laugh when a threat or tension is removed, and safety is re-established.

64

7. *Arousal-suspense-surprise.* People may laugh when there is a slow buildup of suspense during the telling of a story or joke. This laughter is considered an expression of the tension combined with the knowledge that it is "just a story."

8. *Ambivalence.* People may laugh when experiencing uncertainty about what to do, say, feel, or choose. This laughter is displayed *during* the felt ambivalence.

These explanations for why people laugh help to explain why teachers may encounter and be baffled by such a variety of student reactions to class humor. Evidently, the humor *stimulus* is not the only factor to consider. As the theories of humor suggest, the "invisible" conditions in which the student finds himself or herself affect the response to the teacher's humor. Reactions to humor generally are categorized in four ways: (1) release of tension (catharsis), (2) increase of tension, (3) promotion of positive feelings, regard, and inclusion, and (4) promotion of negative feelings, exclusion, and defensiveness.

This description of the theories and effects of humor must also be tempered by another consideration for teachers: the level of student knowledge and sophistication about the content. Humor is a cognitive act. In order for teacher humor to be understood and appreciated, students must first understand the content of the humorous stimulus. The incongruity thesis illustrates this factor most directly. If a student does not understand that incongruity exists at the outset, how can humorous resolution of that situation be achieved? On several occasions when observing colleagues teaching, I have found a teacher to be quite humorous, although reactions from the students have not been appreciative. In part (and without attributing fault to the students only), I speculate that the students either have insufficient knowledge of the necessary context or lack the sophistication to understand the professor's humorous touch. Other explanations might be an established hostile or apathetic climate in the class (Martineau, 1972), or variations in student levels of interest, energy, and listening behavior.

Humor: Attraction, Anxiety, and Power

Research on humor as a communication tool suggests its connections to three broad areas of study: attraction, anxiety, and power. These are social-psychological processes operating in many interpersonal interactions, including those in the classroom.

Humor and Attraction. It has been observed that without a sense of humor, our world would be intolerable (Allen, 1981). Humor is a major force and a needed one for dealing with the real world. Perhaps students have a valid point when they complain about classes not being part of the real world—the real world is filled with humor but all too often humor is excluded from the world of teaching and learning.

A concept formed by anthropologists in the mid-1900s (Radcliffe-Brown, 1940) is relevant here: the *joking relationship*. Joking relationships are those in which two persons who share a close relationship tease and joke each other, seeming unrelentless at times, without taking offense. The interpretations of joking relationship behavior are mixed. "Tension-release" theories (Freud, [1905] 1960; Brandes, 1980) hold that an undercurrent of tension is inherent in any close relationship and is released through the joking. "Play" theorists (Kennedy, 1970; Howell, 1973) argue that affection and goodwill motivate the humor, which in turn develops increased trust and interpersonal bonding. Both theories surely operate in a classroom.

Yet students who are uncertain of the teacher's motives may opt for cautious reactions to teacher-initiated humor. Perhaps because teacher humor is infrequent in the classroom, its use may be perceived with puzzlement by students: "Why is the teacher trying to be funny?" "Is the teacher laughing *at* me or *with* me?" "I don't think the teacher's attempts at humor are funny, but I'll laugh anyway because I don't want to get on the teacher's bad side. After all, I'm hoping to get at least a B in this course."

These student comments about teacher humor suggest uncertainty about the relational base shared with the teacher and concern about being accepted as part of the class group. As Martineau (1972) has explained so well, humor (whether derogatory or esteeming) affects the morale and behavior of the groups involved. Students do want to be perceived as a positive part of the social structure of the classroom.

Teachers also seek positive regard from their students. While findings on the effect of humor in increasing student comprehension and retention are mixed (Gruner, 1985; Kaplan and Pascoe, 1977), students generally report greater enjoyment of instruction that incorporates humor and wit (Zillman and Bryant, 1983). Perceptions of speaker credibility indicate higher ratings on the dimensions of likeability and competence when humor is included in the message. On the other hand, Darling and Civikly concluded that "Humor that is not perceived as open, honest, and spontaneous may be more destructive to the communicative climate than an absence of humor" (1984, p. 804).

Humor and Anxiety. In 1905, one of the earliest analyses of humor was published, Sigmund Freud's *Jokes and Their Relation to the Unconscious.* Freud contended that humor in most cases is a display of such taboo behaviors as aggression, sexual desire, and fear. Any of these feelings may exist in the classroom. Humor also has been identified with the ending of anxiety or the resolution of an ambiguous situation—also situations possible in the classroom. Humor manifests itself for some people in times of heightened stress or crisis—situations also relevant to the classroom. The point to be remembered is that the humor displayed by teachers and students can have a wide range of motivations and arouse an equally wide range of responses.

In a study of the effect of teacher humor on classroom climate, Darling and Civikly (1984) concluded that without establishment of a relational base, teacher humor is perceived as more defense-arousing than supportive and may be more detrimental than the use of no humor. The authors suggest that the social structure of the classroom contributes to the students' defensive reactions. Playful teacher humor may provoke defensiveness because the nature of the humor contradicts student expectations for the teacher's controlling role. Recent research on teasing (Dallinger and Prince, 1984) found 100 percent accuracy in interpretation of teasing that was intended by the teaser as negative but only 65 percent accuracy when the teasing was intended as positive. Unless the relational base is developed, the teacher's effort to incorporate humor or teasing in instruction may be counterproductive. In my own teaching, when I realize that my teasing or playing with the students has little or no response, I gently remind them that I would not do so unless I felt positively about them. Such an instance is a good signal that while the teacher may feel positive and secure with the students, the students may be less sure of that relational base.

Student expectations based on the instructor's gender and sex-role behaviors should also be taken into consideration in the study of humor and teaching. Darling and Civikly (1984) found that students responded defensively to female instructors who used aggressive humor and to male instructors who used non-aggressive humor. These two uses of humor contradict traditional social expectations for men and women (Civikly, 1983); in such cases, reactions of suspicion and defensiveness are not uncommon.

Humor and Power. College classrooms are social structures with an identifiable power hierarchy of professors, teaching assistants, and students. Research on social status and humor (Coser, 1959) suggests the existence of a corresponding humor hierarchy in which the higher-status person initiates the humor and the lower-status person is expected to laugh and appreciate the humor. It has also been found that when the lower-status figure is with others of the same status, humor against the higher status figure is a common event, probably serving as a means of asserting a sense of desired power (Zillman and Cantor, 1972).

Interpersonal power, whether destructive or constructive, incorporates issues of influence, persuasion, and credibility. *Destructive power* appears in the superiority humor of putdowns, sarcasm that is directed at a person, ethnic humor, and sexist humor. Goodchilds (1959) found that a group member with a sarcastic wit was perceived as possessing interpersonal power but was not well liked. A "clown" was well liked but was perceived as having little power to influence other group members. It appears that some balance of these two modes is desirable for college instructors. *Constructive power* can be displayed in various forms of humor and instruction. As noted earlier, the mastery theory of humor suggests a form of power as does the use of humor and wit to elicit ratings of high credibility (Tamborini and Zillman, 1981). Humor also serves as a social corrective and can be an effective persuasive tool to hint at or evoke desired changes. When joking rather than direct threat is used to enforce norms, the negative side effects of a direct hostile confrontation are often avoided.

Humor also displays itself in research on group interaction and leadership. Individuals identified as popular and selected as group leaders often include those who have demonstrated a sense of humor. At times when tensions can stall or halt a class's productivity, humor is quite useful in restoring a productive atmosphere. Research on characteristics of class clowns during early adolescence (Damico and Purkey, 1978) suggests that these students are not merely troublemakers to the teachers. Class clowns display such leadership qualities as being active, assertive, popular, independent, and creative. Damico and Purkey compare these traits with those of adult wits: "Among adults, groups containing wits were found to possess higher morale, be more task-oriented, and better at solving problems than groups without wits. . . . Given the similarity between adolescent clowns and adult wits in other areas, it is safe to assume that clowns might make similar contributions to groups within schools" (p. 397).

Incorporating Humor into Teaching

To date, the research findings about the use of humor in college instruction are disappointing, in that they often contradict teachers' and students' gut-level feeling that humor is a reliable and consistently positive force in teaching. I share in that disappointment but am optimistic in explaining such findings. Most studies have isolated the humor stimulus but have failed to establish and identify the relational base existing between teacher and students—a much more difficult task.

As discussed earlier, the teacher's role in establishing a relational base involves accumulation of information about the students in the class. At the same time, the teacher's own philosophical stance on the role of humor in teaching must not be ignored. The following questions should clarify the teacher's belief structure.

- Does the teacher enjoy teaching and students, or are resentments about instructional responsibilities and interactions displayed?
- Is humor appropriate, necessary, or important to classroom instruction?
- Is the teacher willing to take the time and energy to learn about the students in the class so that the humor used will be relevant to that group?

- Is the teacher comfortable using humor?
- Does the teacher worry about loss of control of the class, negative impression, or loss of the superior teacher role?
- Does the teacher promote a safe class environment in which all participants can display humor?
- Does the teacher provide students with sufficient knowledge before using related humor?

It follows from the relational base premise that there are no foolproof cookbook recipes for using humor effectively. Each teacher and student is different and each class is different. The creative mix of the classroom group with humor is evidenced by reported flops when an instructor tells the same story in two different classes and encounters disparate reactions.

However, we are not left with an impossible task. Five general guidelines can direct the usage and evaluation of teacher humor.

1. *Review and assess how humor has been used in the class.* Placement of a tape recorder in an unobtrusive location while teaching can provide excellent feedback.

2. *Analyze and assess the classroom atmosphere.* Each class develops norms and relational bases distinctive to itself.

3. *Identify humor styles comfortable to you.* There is a wide range of choices from which to select: stories and anecdotes, puns, riddles, limericks, cartoons and visuals, understatement and exaggeration, impersonation, mime, teasing, satire, witticisms, jokes on oneself, and political humor.

4. *Work on "planned spontaneity" of instructional humor.* This involves doing some preparation of examples and incidents relevant and humorous to the students, then presenting these in a "spontaneous" manner.

5. *Evaluate the humor developed and used.* Watch for student reactions and ask for feedback regarding their interest, attention, liking, and comprehension of the material presented in lectures and discussions. Use this feedback to direct use of humor in class and to refine any rough edges that may be identified.

Specific application of these guidelines can take many forms. Several that I have used or observed include amusing anecdotes, comments that compliment the class as being competent and smart, characterization or impersonation of individuals, exaggeration, and teasing. Other applications are described by Baughman (1979) and Wandersee (1982). Without much effort, amusing and witty quotes or visual inserts can be included in such standard teaching routines as board work, handouts, transparencies, syllabi, demonstrations, recitations, case studies, and lab worksheets. In developing these materials, it has been found that humorous response is maximized when the insert or challenge is difficult enough but not too difficult as to present an interminable struggle. If too little cognitive challenge is provided, student perceptions of the material (and possibly the instructor) may be a combination of bland, silly, mundane, and ingratiating impressions (Zigler, Levine, and Gould, 1967).

Since humor encourages a reciprocal response, teacher humor is likely to instigate clever responses from students. Their creation of such responses requires mental alertness and activity—qualities to be welcomed in the classroom. In addition to making learning a more enjoyable experience, the use of appropriate humor is a way to change the tempo or tone of the class, lessen student apathy, develop a sense of class cohesion and identity, communicate respect for the students' intelligence, and express positive regard for their presence and participation.

Classrooms do have unequal social structures. Role distinctions are expected and accepted as part of the classroom culture. Humor can respect these differences *and* serve to promote the cohesive and positive dimensions of the class group. A quote from D. H. Lawrence (Moore, 1962, pp. 770-771) appears in each of my course syllabi and is posted on my office door: "So long as there's a bit of a laugh going, things are all right. As soon as this infernal seriousness, like a greasy sea, heaves up, everything is lost."

Quality teaching need not be a greasy sea.

References

Allen, S. *Funny People.* New York: Stein and Day, 1981.

Baughman, M. D. "Teaching with Humor: A Performing Art." *Contemporary Education,* 1979, *51* (1), 26-30.

Brandes, S. *Metaphors of Masculinity.* Philadelphia: University of Pennsylvania Press, 1980.

Civikly, J. M. "A Comparison of Male and Female Uses of Humor Types and Humor Functions." Paper presented at the International Communication Association Conference, Dallas, May 29, 1983.

Coser, R. L. "Some Social Functions of Laughter." *Human Relations,* 1959, *12,* 171-182.

Dallinger, J. M., and Prince, N. "Teasing: Goals and Responses." Paper presented at the Speech Communication Association Conference, Chicago, November, 1984.

Damico, S. B., and Purkey, W. W. "Class Clowns: A Study of Middle School Students." *American Educational Research Journal,* 1978, *15* (3), 391-398.

Darling, A. L., and Civikly, J. M. "The Effect of Teacher Humor on Classroom Climate." In *Improving University Teaching, Contributed Papers,* Tenth International Conference, Vol. III, College Park, Md., 1984, 798-805.

Freud, S. *Jokes and Their Relation to the Unconscious.* New York: Norton, 1960. (Originally published 1905.)

Goodchilds, J. D. "Effects of Being Witty on Position in the Social Structure of a Small Group." *Sociometry,* 1959, *22,* 261-272.

Gruner, C. R. "Advice to the Beginning Speaker on Using Humor—What the Research Tells Us." *Communication Education,* 1985, *34,* 142-147.

Highet, G. *The Art of Teaching.* New York: Random House (Vintage), 1950.

Howell, R. W. *Teasing Relationships.* Reading, Mass.: Addison-Wesley, 1973.

Kaplan, R. M., and Pascoe, G. C. "Humorous Lectures and Humorous Examples: Some Effects upon Comprehension and Retention." *Journal of Educational Psychology*, 1977, *69* (1), 61–65.

Kennedy, J. G. "Bonds of Laughter among the Tarahumara Indians." In W. Goldschmidt and H. Hoijer (Eds.), *Social Anthropology of Latin America: Essays in Honor of Ralph Leon Beals*. Berkeley, Calif.: University of California Press, 1970.

Koestler, A. *The Act of Creation*. New York: Dell, 1964.

Martineau, W. H. "A Model of the Social Functions of Humor." In J. H. Goldstein and P. E. McGhee (Eds.), *The Psychology of Humor*. New York: Academic Press, 1972.

Moore, H. T. (Ed.) *The Collected Letters of D. H. Lawrence*. Volume 2. New York: Viking Press, 1962.

Radcliffe-Brown, A. R. "On Joking Relationships." *Africa*, 1940, *13*, 195–210.

Rosenfeld, L. B. "Communication Climate and Coping Mechanisms in the College Classroom." *Communication Education*, 1983, *32* (2), 167–174.

Tamborini, R., and Zillman, D. "College Students' Perceptions of Lectures Using Humor." *Perceptual and Motor Skills*, 1981, *52*, 427–432.

Wandersee, J. H. "Humor as a Teaching Strategy." *American Biology Teacher*, 1982, *44* (4), 212–218.

Zigler, E., Levine, J., and Gould, L. "Cognitive Challenge as a Factor in Children's Humor Appreciation." *Journal of Personality and Social Psychology*, 1967, *6*, 332–336.

Zillman, D., and Bryant, J. "Uses and Effects of Humor in Educational Ventures." In P. E. McGhee and J. H. Goldstein (Eds.), *Handbook of Humor Research*, (Vol. II: Applied Studies). New York: Springer-Verlag, 1983.

Zillman, D., and Cantor, J. R. "Directionality of Transitory Dominance as a Communication Variable Affecting Humor Appreciation." *Journal of Personality and Social Psychology*, 1972, *24*, 191–198.

Ziv, A. *Personality and Sense of Humor*. New York: Springer Publishing Co., 1984.

Jean M. Civikly is associate professor of Speech Communication at the University of New Mexico. In addition to her teaching and research on the interpersonal dynamics of classroom instruction, she is director of the university's Teaching Assistant Resource Center.

*Classrooms can serve as laboratories for experimenting
with collaboration rather than win-lose conflict styles.
For conflict management, the process is the product.*

Teacher-Student Confrontations

Joyce L. Hocker

College teachers have always experienced conflicts with their students,
both inside and outside of class, and recent years have been no exception.
While most teachers expect that teaching and learning will take place in a
cooperative atmosphere, struggles and conflicts inevitably occur. They
present challenges for practicing what we preach. Their resolution shapes
one's teaching style.

The Nature of Conflict in the Teacher-Student Relationship

In a typical interaction between teacher and student, a student questions a grade on a paper:

> *Student:* Could I talk with you about my grade on the first paper?
> *Professor:* Sure, come on in.
> *Student:* I'd like to know your criteria for an A. I worked really
> hard and thought I'd written an A paper.
> *Professor:* Well, it was a good paper, but it had some flaws. For
> instance, you had a lot of proofreading errors and you didn't
> follow the assignment fully. [Explains]

J. M. Civikly, (Ed.). *Communicating in College Classrooms.*
New Directions for Teaching and Learning, no. 26. San Francisco: Jossey-Bass, June 1986.

Student: I didn't know we had to use outside sources.
Professor: I covered that in class. You must have missed it.
Student: Oh. Well, thanks.
Professor: Sure, any time.

The professor will likely assume that the above interaction was a routine inquiry about a grade, in which the student went away satisfied. The student might report to friends that the professor was unclear in class, unfair in applying standards, inconsistent in interpretation of requirements, did not read the paper carefully, or conducted the interview in an arrogant, demeaning manner. For the professor, no important conflict may have occurred; for the student, who may be boiling inside, the episode might be considered "a serious conflict."

Students report more personal involvement in their conflicts with teachers than do teachers; they view tactics used by professors as authoritarian, coercive, and highly powerful (Jamieson and Thomas, 1974). In fact, when students were asked to describe the most negative experiences in their lives (Branon, 1972), one-third mentioned negative interpersonal relations with teachers. During the past decade, students in my conflict management classes have consistently identified interactions with teachers as a sample conflict in which they felt they had little power. Common content areas include the student's trying to get a grade changed or disagreeing with teaching methods or class requirements (Wilmot, 1976), personal conflicts such as wanting to be closer to the teacher, and conflicts over the teacher's time and availability, direction of research, and deadlines.

Students also remember conflicts with teachers as unproductive or even destructive. Almost all students report that they talked, argued, or disagreed with their teachers once. When they were unsuccessful at reaching their goal, they gave up. In one study (Wilmot, 1976), no students mentioned talking to the instructor more than once or expanding their conflict management tactics to include coalition formation or third-party intervention—one exchange with the professor was apparently all they felt safe enough to manage. Most teacher-student conflicts, as reported by students, can be characterized as win-lose, with the conflict being managed through high-powered coercive tactics. According to students, teachers typically escalate the conflict, then use their power over students to force them to back down. Students report feeling anxious, dumb, frustrated, angry, misunderstood, annoyed, hostile, uncomfortable, unsure, helpless, disturbed, mad, sorry, and revengeful (Wilmot, 1976).

The purpose of this chapter is to present typical issues that arise in conflicts inside and outside the classroom, information for analysis of the conflicts, and suggestions for managing them in such a way as to model a process of collaboration rather than reinforcing the win-lose model of conflict management. The reduction of tiresome, predictable, and unproductive conflicts can make the teaching enterprise more energizing instead of draining and can teach students that educated people can work *with* instead of *against* each other. Additionally, teachers who have learned to manage disputes often involve themselves with their students rather than take refuge behind traditional authority roles.

For the purpose of this discussion, conflict will be presented as "an expressed struggle, between at least two interdependent parties, who perceive incompatible goals, scarce rewards, and interference from the other party in achieving their goals" (Hocker and Wilmot, 1985, p. 23). Conflict is present whenever it is communicated, verbally or nonverbally. Conflict includes both content and relationship issues. *Content* issues have to do with the specific subject or information defining the struggle (in the case above, the grade on the paper). *Relationship* issues have to do with who the conflicting parties are in relation to each other—who has more power, who can define the terms, who can choose the tactics, how each will respond to the moves of the other, and whether either party will allow the other to influence them in any way. Content goals can be observed by outsiders to the conflict, whereas relationship goals make sense only in the context of the specific relationship. Usually, the relationship issues arouse more feelings than do the content issues. In the above example, the student may have been implying that the teacher should take responsibility for the lack of clarity experienced by the student, but the teacher tacitly refused to do so. The teacher's relational message may have been, "I did a good job explaining; your performance is your responsibility." The struggle involved a relational issue of responsibility, not only the content issue of the grade, and *both* are real issues.

Conflict can serve as a basis for both productive and destructive activity, depending on how the parties handle their differences. The Chinese ideograph for conflict combines images of danger and opportunity. In the Western world, however, most images that come to mind when the word "conflict" is mentioned are negative, such as anger, hostility, war, tension, destruction, and chaos. Seldom do such images as growth, change, challenge, rebirth, and opportunity come quickly to mind. Yet teachers can learn from conflicts as well as students can, to the betterment of teaching style and understanding of the impact on students. If teachers can learn to move toward situations of conflict for the purpose of understanding and resolution, instead of away from the person who brings conflict into awareness, learning can result from what often begins as a painful and stressful experience.

Productive conflicts. Have you ever experienced a positive, productive conflict with students? If so, you probably learned something, made adjustments in your own communication patterns, and solved a problem. Additionally, you may have felt a sense of heightened trust with the students, more liking for them, and a positive assessment of your own abilities as a communicator. The goals of any productive conflict are to *solve the immediate problem* represented in the conflict and to *enhance the interpersonal relationship* to the extent that such is needed to continue working together. If the problem is solved, but the relationship worsens, the conflict is not settled. Following is a sample of dialogue that might transform the previous case into one that will end productively:

> *Student:* [After formalities] I thought I understood what to do on the paper. I followed the assignment.
> *Teacher:* Tell me your understanding of the paper assignment.
> *Student:* [Does so]
> *Teacher:* I think I see where the problem is. Let's trace back where the confusion came from.

In the replay of the grade conflict scenario, the teacher began to transform the conflict into a potentially productive one by increasing interdependence (working together to trace the root of the conflict), by refusing to define the grade as a scarce resource, by not blocking the student's goals immediately, and by overtly agreeing that a problem existed. Even if the grade does not change, the student's goal of understanding what went wrong will be reached. In all conflicts, the parties must have enough power to solve their problem and enough self-esteem to communicate openly and effectively. The problems of powerlessness and low esteem are core issues in every conflict.

Teachers' Conflict Management Styles

Recently, a professor reported to me an unsatisfactory thesis defense meeting during which the graduate student presented an unacceptable plan for his research. The professor reported the meeting's closing dialogue:

> *Student:* So what do you want me to do to make it acceptable?
> *Professor:* If you don't know that by now, I don't know why we are having this meeting. Produce a valid and reliable design and then I'll see if it's okay.

This student and professor were using two different styles for their conflict, styles which were learned as reasonable (if not desirable) for that situation (Schuetz, 1975). Conflict styles are not an inherent part of the personality; rather, they are learned as people encounter life experiences which put them into conflict. The purpose of analyzing one's conflict management style is not to discover underlying personality dynamics but to gain information about what one's repertoire of styles contains.

If one had as models professors who were imperious and demanding but rigorous and fair, one might try to emulate that style in class. If one learned from professors who were empathic and concerned about the personal growth of their students, a different style of conflict might develop. You can expand or modify your conflict style if you notice repeated unproductive conflicts in which you or the student consistently lose esteem, credibility, composure, trust, desired information, or other tangible or intangible losses, such as time.

Five conflict styles can be identified for purposes of analysis. The diagram shown in Figure 1, modified from the work of Kilmann and Thomas (1975), presents the five styles in terms of concern for one's own goals and concern for the other and the relationship.

Each style can be used effectively at some time, depending on the problem and needs of the people. Most professors, one may safely assert, overuse competition and avoidance with their students. As noted in Figure 1, both *competition*, which structures the conflict so that one pursues one's own concerns at the expense of the other, and *avoidance*, characterized by passive, nonassertive behavior, share a common dimension: Both communicate little concern for the other party and for the relationship. The *accommodation* style involves giving in to the other. The concern for the other

Figure 1. Conflict Styles

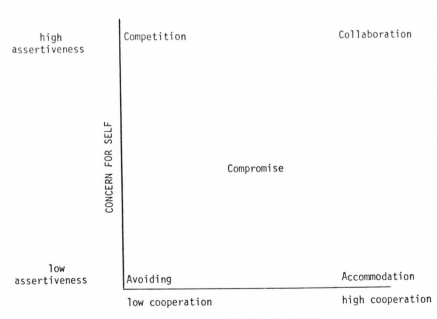

party and for the relationship is high, but concern for one's own goals is low. *Compromise* is a style highly endorsed by American culture and often works well, since concern for self, other, and the relationship are moderate. However, compromise can often be an "easy out" that does not use the problem-solving abilities of the parties. *Collaboration* shows high concern for the self, for the other, and for the relationship. It is a cooperative, highly involving style, producing solutions that are likely to be accepted by all parties and serve as genuine conflict resolutions (Hocker and Wilmot, 1985). In the example of the thesis meeting, the student used the accommodation style, while the professor used competition. The power structure encouraged the use of these particular styles, but they will most likely produce continued frustration and denigration ("He's a shoddy researcher," or "He's completely impossible to work for").

Your own style of managing conflict can be assessed in several ways. (1) During class evaluations ask students to answer the question, "Comment on my way of handling conflicts with students inside and outside of class." (2) Fill out the Putnam-Wilson Conflict Behavior Scale (1982), which gives information on three styles: solution-orientation, nonconfrontation, and control orientation, which subsume some of the Thomas-Kilmann styles into a validated research instrument. (3) Think back over troubling episodes that seem to happen over and over with your students. One example might be going over a test with the class. Often such sessions, while they provide immediate learning of content material, leave professor and students unsatisfied or even angry. The professor may be on the defensive and thus adopt a competitive style to cope with the demands of the situation. The students may see competition as the only way they can gain points on the quiz and persist in trying to prove a test item to be incorrectly scored or poorly written. A collaborative style can grow from focusing on concepts, making decisions about items in private, and asking students to expand on their questions.

Many people rate themselves as more solution-oriented than others, especially those who have less power, such as students. In the thesis meeting example, the student probably would rate the professor as interested in control, not solutions. The higher-powered party usually tries to remain less involved than the lower-powered party and therefore uses fewer collaborative tactics.

Power Struggles

Power hierarchies exist in all classes. Even professors who model humane and effective teaching use power with students, since they structure the learning environment and, to a large extent, the kinds of conflicts that students may initiate. One undergraduate student reported his assessment of the power structure: "The power difference between us was nothing less than awesome. I was merely a first quarter freshman and he was "A PROFESSOR." Also, his mastery of the spoken word was vastly superior to mine, and he intimidated me with it" (quoted in Wilmot, 1976).

However, professors do not hold all the power (Raven and French, 1956; Hocker and Wilmot, 1985), since students have value in the educational system as people and as consumers of the service provided by their teachers. If professors had no students, or hostile, inattentive students, they could not do their work effectively.

Power currencies are areas upon which you may draw to persuade the other party to deal effectively with you in a conflict situation. The concept of currencies depends on the idea that power is a product of the *relationship*, not the individual person. "All power in interpersonal relations is a property of the social relationship rather than a quality of the individual outside of the relationship" (Hocker and Wilmot, 1985, p. 76). Emerson (1962) posited that person A has power over person B to the extent that B is dependent on A for goal attainment, and vice versa. To illustrate this point, think of a college student who is trying to enroll in a class listed as closed. To determine the professor's power over the student, we must know (1) the student's goal (to add the class) and (2) how dependent the student is on the professor in accomplishing the goal (completely). To decide the student's power to negotiate with the professor we must know (1) the professor's goals (have a full but not overloaded class and to appear reasonable) and (2) the professor's dependency on the student (slight). In this case the professor controls more of the resources, but the student does have some negotiating power based on the professor's goals. The student's best argument would center around a flexible definition of "a full class" and an appeal to fairness.

Currencies frequently drawn upon in conflicts include: expertise; control of resources such as attention, time and knowledge; linkages to other people in the system, such as other professors or the business community; personal qualities of attractiveness, warmth, conversational skills, or status; and intimacy or caring (Hocker and Wilmot, 1985). Students usually underestimate their power with professors, unaware of the value of persistence in asking for clarification without attacking.

For productive conflict management to occur, power must be at least temporarily balanced. Professors can voluntarily limit their power by avoiding the use of threats and structuring ways for students to influence the teaching process. Occasionally, they can use the services of a third party such as a chair or dean when the student cannot speak for him/ herself effectively. Teachers, usually in the high-powered position, can take charge of the collaborative process for the good of all parties.

In the thesis meeting scenario, the professor could have said something like this when the student asked, "What do you want me to do?"

Professor: I want you and the committee to end up with a project that can be published and that we can all be proud of, especially you. I see some problems with getting there the way the design is now structured. I think what you want is [gives specific suggestions]. If you'll drop by an outline of rewrites, I'll give you some initial reaction about whether it solves the problem.

Conflict Tactics

How to drive your students crazy. Conflict tactics are the specific choices people make in managing their conflicts. Certain tactics continue to give teachers the high-powered advantage and underline the dependent position of students. Tactics guaranteed to drive a particular conflict underground instead of dealing with it openly would be teacher comments such as, "That's just the way life is," "Too bad," "Let me tell you what you should do," "This is a bad class," and other insensitive assertions. Students report a high level of frustration when the teacher interrupts them constantly in class, forgets commitments, gives vague answers, ignores requests, answers only part of a question, answers in an overly abstract manner, makes hostile jokes, gives ambivalent answers, or avoids a student altogether. These *avoidance* tactics (Hocker and Wilmot, 1985; Sillars and others, 1982), help to keep the power structure unbalanced.

Instead of avoiding the conflict, teachers can engage in a conflict, either in competitive or collaborative ways. Students receive little help from teachers who find fault with what they have done, make hostile jokes at the students' expense, mind-read, or issue threats. These tactics can be classified as *competitive* tactics. A list of *collaborative* tactics follows, along with examples of their use in teacher-student conflicts:

1. *Description.* "I noticed that your grades have declined for the past three quarters," *not* "You must not have been working."

2. *Disclosure.* "You don't have any way to know this, but past experience leads me to conclude that students have trouble finishing incompletes. So I am fairly prejudiced against the practice," *not* "You'll never finish it."

3. *Negative inquiry* (soliciting complaints about self). "You said you were disappointed with the class. What makes you say that? I'd like to know," *not* "You should have read the syllabus more carefully."

4. *Emphasizing common interests.* "I know both of us are interested in your doing well in the course. How are you studying for the exams?" *not* "I can't help you if you don't study."

Collaboration as a strategy of conflict management builds on constructive conflict management tactics. Personalities do not need changing—the communication people choose to use needs changing.

Collaborative Goals

For collaborators, conflict presents the opportunity for the student and professor to learn from the process of negotiating content and relationship; the process is the product. When teachers treat every conflict over a grade the same way, they communicate a high-powered, non-caring form of conflict management. *If collaboration guides the conflict management process, new participants make this situation a new conflict.* An appropriate way to approach the conflict would be to ask, "What would be the best course of action at this time, with this student, given the constraints of the situation, and given my feelings and opinions?"

Principled negotiation. Fisher and Ury's popular book, *Getting To Yes* (1981), describes steps for conflict management that emphasize the process rather than the outcome of the conflict situation. Teachers can learn the four principles of this approach and apply them to teacher-student conflicts. Conflicts handled in this manner are likely to be characterized by the concerns discussed so far—humanism, process, relationship goals, and shared power. They can be remembered by the words *People, Interests, Options,* and *Criteria.*

A teacher in a large university discovered that one of his carefully constructed multiple-choice tests had made its way to the files of various student groups. At first, he was enraged and devised a plan to drop the test review, make up a new test, and grade on a rigorous curve. Then he thought about just forgetting the "leak" and going on with the test. His conflict was not with an individual student, since he did not know who was responsible for the stolen test, but with an amorphous group of students who did not know he was aware of the theft. Using Fisher and Ury's four steps, the professor worked his way through the problem:

1. *Separate people from the problem.* Giving the same test would be unfair to the students not having access to the files. Not all the students created the problem, so an unfair solution would penalize every student.

2. *Focus on interests, not positions.* Rather than making position statements or non-negotiable demands, interest bargaining encourages development of overlapping concerns. The teacher's interest in this conflict involved having students learn the material, refusing to reward students who stole the test, refusing to punish students who did not steal the test, and avoiding a time-consuming task of completely remaking the test. The students' interest involved fair testing and grading and a test review. Usually, interests can be made to overlap, and the solution can be drawn from the area of overlap.

3. *Generate a variety of options.* Often, the first choice that pops into one's mind is one that reflects anger, hostility, defeat, revenge, or fuzzy thinking. In the case of the purloined exam, a first choice might be,

"Give an essay exam" (too hard to grade), "Let it go" (unfair option), or "Make up a rigorous new test" (time-consuming). The more options that can be generated by all parties, the better. In this case, the professor asked the undergraduate board of students to help him come up with options that met shared criteria.

4. *Develop criteria for judging solutions.* Insist that the result be based on some objective standard of judgment. In this case, the criteria might include the professor's time, fairness to the non-thieving students, professional standards, moral standards, equal treatment, or precedent. Many other possible criteria exist for different conflicts. Choose the criteria for judgment *before* choosing the particular solution.

With the help of undergraduates not in his class, the professor revised the order of test questions so that a pre-marked answer sheet could not be used, changed some but not all of the questions, and added more questions on lecture material. He was satisfied that the solution met the criteria set earlier. People, Interests, Options, and Criteria can be applied to any conflict in which parties wish to collaborate for a high-quality solution.

Patterns of Conflict Interaction

By this time, you may have identified predictable patterns of conflict between you and your students. You might want to list kinds of recurring events. If your students consistently turn in late work, you might try to identify the communication structure you use. Do you communicate threats? Do you fail to give a clear description of expectations? Do you give answers that students would label "ambiguous"? Do you expect the students to do projects they are not trained to do? Before assuming that you have irresponsible students or that you are doing something wrong, analyze the communication you use. Recurring events give clues about the nature of ongoing conflicts.

Fractionating Conflicts

Fractionating conflicts refers to the process of sizing a dispute appropriately or breaking it down from one large mass to several smaller, more manageable conflicts. For example, if angry students ask you to explain you grading policy, ask "What do you want to hear about specifically?" This response sizes the dispute downward, rather than setting up a potentially defensive situation in which the professor explains grading philosophy in general. The following phrases help with fractionation (Hocker and Wilmot, 1985): "What part of that problem is most important to you right now?" "Who are the people most immediately involved?" "I want to hear more about your objections. Please start with the most important."

Use of Third Party

Sometimes, in spite of the best efforts of teacher and student, the conflict remains at an impasse and the services of a third party must be sought. The chair of the department, dean, or student complaint board should be used only when two-party negotiations have failed—never as an avoidance device. The same kinds of skills discussed previously lead to successful third-party negotiations. (See Hocker and Wilmot, 1985, for a detailed treatment of third-party intervention.)

Conclusion

Effective conflict management begins with a change in one's way of dealing with conflict, including understanding its nature, styles developed over time, power in conflicts, collaborative goals, and fractionation. Productive conflict management inside and outside the classroom provides the opportunity to model the process of working *with* instead of *against* others. The use of power presents a paradoxical situation. To be effective people, we need to take advantage of opportunities and use resources. Yet, within an ongoing relationship, maximization of individual power is counterproductive for all parties. Learning to pursue peaceful relations with opposing parties may be the central issue of our times, and the classroom could be the ideal training ground for honing these skills.

References

Branon, J. M. "Negative Human Interaction." *Journal of Counseling Psychology,* 1972, *19* (1), 81–89.

Emerson, R. M. "Power-dependence Relations." *American Sociological Review,* 1962, *27,* 31–41.

Fisher, R., and Ury, W. *Getting to Yes: Negotiating Agreement Without Giving In.* Boston: Houghton Mifflin, 1981.

Hocker, J. L., and Wilmot, W. W. *Interpersonal Conflict.* (2nd ed.) Dubuque, Iowa: Wm. C. Brown, 1985.

Jamieson, D. W., and Thomas, K. W. "Power and Conflict in the Student-Teacher Relationship." *Journal of Applied Behavioral Science,* 1974, *10,* 321–333.

Kilmann, R., and Thomas, K. "Interpersonal Conflict-Handling Behavior as Reflections of Jungian Personality Dimensions." *Psychological Reports,* 1975, *37,* 971–980.

Putnam, L. L., and Wilson, C. E. "Communicative Strategies in Organizational Conflicts: Reliability and Validity of a Measurement Scale." In M. Burgoon (Ed.), *Communication Yearbook 6.* Beverly Hills, Calif.: Sage, 1982.

Raven, B. H., and French, J. R. P., Jr. "A Formal Theory of Social Power." *Psychological Review,* 1956, *63,* 181–194.

Schuetz, J. E. "A Contingent Model of Argumentation Based on a Game Theory Paradigm." Unpublished doctoral dissertation, University of Colorado, 1975.

82

Sillars, A. L., Coletti, S. F., and Rogers, M. A. "Coding Verbal Conflict Tactics: Nonverbal and Perceptual Correlates of the 'Avoidance-Distributive-Integrative' Distinction." *Human Communication Research*, 1982, *9* (1), 83–95.

Wilmot, W. W. "The Influence of Personal Conflict Styles of Teachers on Student Attitudes Toward Conflict." Paper presented at the International Communication Association Conference, Portland, Oregon, April 15, 1976.

Joyce L. Hocker is associate professor of Interpersonal Communication at the University of Montana. Her research and training interests are conflict management, mediation, family and couple communication, and therapeutic communication.

*In learning as in loving, without regenerative
reciprocity we have only gestures—motions with
no meaning.*

The Art of Teaching:
An Act of Love

Joel M. Jones

In a review of a collection of essays on university teaching, Leslie Fiedler declared that "the encounter of teacher and student is basically an erotic encounter, at best a passionate coming together of strangers, at worst a failed love affair, they confess, lacking the appropriate vocabulary" (1972, p. 65). The time has come to build that vocabulary. When so many in academia applaud a resurgent rationalism, when we read of new converts to the counter-reformation, when the terms "intuitive" and "imaginative," "sensitive," and "subjective" once again take on pejorative connotations, when so many of us (faculty and administrators alike) seem to accept an assumed student passivity, then we need to risk ridicule and parody by developing the vocabulary which will allow us to compare the art of teaching and the act of loving. Both are highly personal communicative arts, which lately have been discussed too often merely in terms of technique. We can move toward the new vocabulary by turning for implicit inspiration to works such as Harold Taylor's *Students Without Teachers* (1969), Kenneth Eble's *A Perfect Education* (1966), Maxine Greene's *Landscapes of Learning* (1978), or Stanford Ericksen's *The Essence of Good Teaching* (1984). For explicit and concrete references, we must turn both to the scattered testimonial statements concerning the erotic nature of teaching-learning and to our own personal classroom experiences.

J. M. Civikly, (Ed.). *Communicating in College Classrooms.*
New Directions for Teaching and Learning, no. 26. San Francisco: Jossey-Bass, June 1986.

Teaching as Loving

To some, the art of teaching seems quite similar to the art of loving. The act of verbal intercourse we call teaching-learning has many parallels with the act of sexual intercourse we call loving. In either act, a few individuals do moderately well some of the time; a few more succeed most of the time; but far too many (pretences and postures aside) merely bumble and stumble their way through all the time. And all this bumbling, stumbling, and fumbling exists in spite of a hyper-abundance of methodology books in both areas, how-to books on teaching and on loving. Repeated too often in our technological society, the word "method" suffers a transmutation from life to death, a mode whereby the mystical becomes mechanical, the communicative word a cleaving sword.

In *Education and Ecstasy* (1968), George Leonard has written convincingly of the ecstasy which should characterize the learning experience at all levels. Kenneth Eble, in *The Aims of College Teaching* (1983) challenges faculty to consider the possibility "that erotic love is both a metaphor for and an actuality of learning" (p. 41). Erotic? Ecstatic? How many of us would describe our educational experience or that of our students in such terms? Far too few, I suspect. Where institutionalized learning of any kind is supposed to be taking place, with at least two parties involved in the communicative discourse, one would hope to find, on the part of each, some feeling for the other. Moreover, the feeling in question should be based on sharing and reciprocal stimulation through voluntary participation; the culmination of the time and energy mutually expended should, on occasion, be characterized as an ecstatic moment. One should *feel*, in profoundly moving ways, those electrifying insights we traditionally call intellectual growth.

Juxtaposed with this ideal image, however, one sees the too-real classroom scene. From nursery to graduate school, teaching could often be characterized as either prostitution—having the saving factor of at least quasi-willing submission by both parties—or rape, the rape of the mind. So often classroom communication seems obligatory, even forced, motivated more by fear than love, a fruitless casting of seed on non-receptive ground, an abortive expenditure of self and subject matter, an academic charade lacking the commitment, conviction, energy and excitement which *both* teacher and student so desperately seek in auditoriums and arenas outside the classroom. To come at the issue more positively, I still envision the act of teaching as an act of love: erotic, ecstatic, expansive—and, of course, enervating, but, finally, energizing. In his observations on master teachers, Joseph Epstein aptly concludes that "Carried out conscientiously, conducted at a high level, conveyed with proper passion, teaching is an arduous task" (1981, p. xi). To communicate as teacher is to commit one's self, body and soul, to a sharing of the mind with students who must be motivated by a recognition of the preparation and passion underlying that commitment.

The Self Transcends Technique

In saying how this is to happen, I am not about to proffer any descriptive-prescriptive method. To do so would be both contradictory and presumptuous. The method of those individuals considered great teachers or great lovers cannot be imitated because it seems inherent to a uniquely personal style. One need only read William Morris' *Effective College Teaching* (1970), Joseph Epstein's *Masters: Portraits of Great Teachers* (1981), or Ken Macrorie's *Twenty Teachers* (1984) to recognize that the styles of successful college teachers are highly individualized. As Joseph Axelrod (1973) stresses in his examination of teaching styles at the university level, "In the end, we shall find that every teacher-artist, like the artist in any sphere, attacks his task in the only way he can: he develops his own style, and he expresses himself in his own personal ways" (p. 9). In teaching, as in loving, the communicative voice and communicated vision seem most effective when personal and therefore cannot be predicated upon arbitrary or absolute methodological principles.

No one can articulate the "right" way. Even Joseph Lowman (1984), in his incisive and important survey of myriad teaching techniques, stresses that the balance of "intellectual excitement" and "interpersonal rapport" will finally be a reflection of personal predisposition and individual character. The technique must reflect the personal touch, the style manifest individual integrity, the "how" evidence the "who." So often, what seems most professional is least personal, hence least authentic. Authenticity comes from being as one is, speaking as one thinks and feels, not from doing as one believes will serve one best professionally. I am reminded of Charles Van Riper's challenge to professors of communication: "Why is it so hard for specialists in the disorders of communication to communicate?" (Macrorie, 1984, p. 114). His specific reference is to the "wretched prose" used by some professors in their professional journals. His essay stresses the need for the personal voice, uncluttered by professional jargon and posturing, if the student is to experience personally the meaning of whatever the professor purports to profess. If our teaching is indeed interpersonal comunication—substantive and significant "penetration" (Altman and Taylor, 1973)—then we cannot simply assume what we see as appropriate professorial postures and throw our words to the wind.

Authenticity Precedes Authority

Though we cannot proffer a simple model for success, there are some generalities which can be posited in developing the parallels between good teaching and loving. The first is the necessity for "exposure." The professor who, when confronting a class, hides behind his or her title, degree, or institutionally-granted position of authority will very likely never engage in ideal communicative interaction. I might not go so far as to agree with a faculty colleague who smilingly suggested that all professors should deliver at least one lecture in the nude. (Granted, this would result in a much higher attendance rate as students awaited the day of "exposure.") On a less dramatic but more essential level, we are simply stressing the need for what Sidney Jourard, in *The Transparent Self* (1964), defines as the "self-disclosure" upon which any authentic and healthy human relationship must be predicated. Too many of us hide behind our literal and figurative sheepskins, expecting or demanding respect for *what* we are institutionally certified to be, not for *who* we are. Whatever abilities and accomplishments the degrees and honorary awards should signify will be discovered by the students sooner or later anyway—and respected much more fully if discovered rather than declared. But if the students have to expend all their energy trying to find the man behind the mask, the woman behind the words, the professing person behind the podium, if they feel forced to respond only to *structured authority* rather than *spontaneous authenticity,* then they may well become the unthinking robots we denounce but too often accept for the sake of classroom comfort and convenience.

Carl Paternite (1983) recently suggested that if we want our students dents to be "active architects of their worlds," if we want them to experience personally the meaning of whatever subject matter we profess, then our teaching must be characterized by an aura of "personalism" which encourages both "risk-taking" and "a high degree of trust" (p. 64). Morris Kline (1977), the internationally distinguished scholar of mathematics, insists that even in a field seen by many as impersonal and objective, effective teaching requires familiarity with the students, as well as with the subject, and a willingness to personalize the teaching-learning process.

My concern for exposure and authenticity should not be construed as an advocacy of the purely confessional mode of discourse. Even the most inexperienced prostitute (along with college teaching, the other ancient profession which usually requires no certification pertinent to the basic occupational act) can tell how shallow and artificial a means of intimacy the confessional voice can be. We are talking, simply, about the same virtues posited by Emerson in his now classic essay of 1837, "The American Scholar": the integration of thinking, feeling, and doing, the synergy of believing and acting, the authenticity of professing a personalized point of view, of defining and sharing one's sense of place in time and space, of using language to explore and to grow rather than to control and constrict, of feeling free to use the pronoun "I"—and to give some substance to it, some basis by which it can take on a social reality, some sense whereby the self can be known and trusted by others. A more con-temporary voice with which Emerson would feel quite comfortable is that of Paulo Freire (1970). No one can dismiss his plea for classroom authen-ticity as sophomoric solipsism or Madison Avenue narcissism. His "stu-dents" are the teachers of the dispossessed in oppressive cultures, but his words apply to any of our classrooms: "One cannot impose oneself, nor even merely co-exist with one's students. . . . Only through communica-tion can human life hold meaning. The teacher's thinking is authenticated only by the authenticity of the students' thinking" (pp. 63-64). And such authenticity of voice, such sharing of personal vision by professor and student, can occur only when one risks one's self to trust in the "other."

Vulnerability Precludes Venerability

Without trust there can be no loving, no learning. As Ken Macrorie has so dramatically revealed in his autobiographical *A Vulnerable Teacher* (1974), where loving and learning are concerned, the process of establishing a trusting relationship can lead to a sense of risk, a feeling of vulnerability on the part of all individuals involved. However, better vulnerable than venerable. Self-styled learned and wise individuals too often speak and listen only to the learned and wise—and, more often than not, end up speaking to only themselves. If we doubt or mistrust the intentions of the person or persons with whom we would relate, we fear the vulnerability so necessary for the communication or communion upon which true learning must be predicated. When fear reigns, the mind freezes and becomes totally self-serving, with only the sense of survival as a paramount priority.

It Takes Two—at Least—to Teach

Peter Elbow, a contributor to the important collection of autobio-graphical reflections called *The New Teachers* (Flournoy, Ed., 1972), is one of the few individuals who has made explicit reference to the sexuality of teaching. "Perhaps my metaphor is too unsavory. But not too sexual. One thing sure is that teaching is sexual. What is uncertain is which practices are natural and which unnatural, which fruitful and which barren. . ." (p. 120). One can only suggest that in our institutions of higher learning the routine monological and masturbatory casting forth of words is little more than the self-serving casting of seed, rather than the dialogic dynamic espoused by communication experts as requisite for learning and loving. In learning as in loving, without regenerative reciprocity we have only gestures—motion with no meaning. There may be 101 or 1001 ways to do it, but if one's way is merely posture or pose, if one remains only a master of technique rather than a servant of touch, the result is an act of no consequence, form with no function, style with little substance.

As Professor Elbow comments, "When the sexuality of teaching is more generally felt and admitted, we may finally draw the obvious moral: the practice should only be performed between consenting adults" (p. 120). With reference to the problem of consent, I suspect there may be proportionately as many professors as students who are unwilling or unwitting victims of cultural conditioning, doing what they must, not what they would. Too often the most professional of professors and prostitutes can convince their "willing" students and patrons that the form of intercourse being purchased is the real thing. But in the calmer moments of reflection, all participants sooner or later recognize that the performance was mechanical, the touching only transitory and illusory.

Less Posture, More Person

The malaise so pervasive in our society often has its basis in our denial of personal self for professional self-interest. We *do* what we should for professional status, but to *be* who we are would better serve our students. With specific reference to the matter of institutional teaching-learning, we condone the objective and neutral and condemn the political and personal. We advocate, in our supposed neutrality, denial of the authentic self for the advancement of the alienated-institutional self (on the part of both teacher and student). However, stressing less the "how" and more the "who," less the procedure and more the person, less the syllabus and more the soul, less the grade and more the growth might lead one closer to the essential though rare eroticism and ecstasy of the finest moments of loving and learning.

At this point in writing the essay, I find myself intimidated by the analogy, embarrassed by the point I am trying to make—feeling forced, even, to apologize for the apparent extremity of what I am saying. One can hear the skeptical reader proclaiming loudly, "This guy is the ultimate educational romantic. The sexuality of teaching—incredible!" But sometimes I look and listen my way around campus for a few days and begin to feel, though identified as an administrator, like a flaming idealist. Every so often, one does find higher learning, the willing moments in which the ecstasy appears, the feeling manifests itself, and one sees two or two hundred individuals engaged in the joy of learning.

There is no need to apologize. Were the metaphor here one of a militaristic bent, were we comparing teaching to the act of making war rather than the act of making love, we would feel no need to apologize for the language, for the lack of sensitivity and sensibility being suggested. As a matter of fact, the metaphor of war might be more appropriate as pure description of what one sees and hears on campus. However, in the prescriptive mode, I will take my stand with the metaphor of sexual love and hope that it will become descriptive for an increasing number of us.

Facing the Realities

I would not suggest that the kind of classroom experience or relationship I advocate herein could or should ever be routine. There are too many factors working against that possibility. For example, were lovers to schedule their sexual encounters for every M-W-F at 10:30 (and never on Sunday) and, in addition, fill out a grade sheet to record their progress, I have my doubts as to how long the ecstasy would prevail. So many of our institutional realities—schedules, syllabi, exams, grades—run contrary to the kind of experience I am describing, but they need not preclude it.

As a teacher, I have gone through weeks when my classroom experience seemed light-years away from the erotic or the ecstatic. Sometimes I have had seminars or classes when such moments occurred only once or twice. The size of the class, in my own experiences, has little to do with it. A graduate seminar several years ago with just eight participants was deadly: I was trying too hard, sometimes being too pushy, other times too passive, continually frustrated, with great expectations and few excitations. Work which should have been fun was usually labor. And when you have to labor at it—when you have to work in the sense of driving or forcing yourself and the other—pain and violation are quite likely to be the consequences. My retrospective diagnosis of that seminar has focused on the fact that the level of *trust* was low, the level of manipulation high.

Several years ago, though, an undergraduate class of over one hundred and forty students (billed and conducted as a "seminar") provided nothing but sheer pleasure, three hours a day, four days a week, for a month. (It was offered during a January mini-mester.) Nearly all of the participants had been students in other classes of mine; most had shared prior classes with others in the "seminar." Sometimes they would lead me, sometimes I them; sometimes one segment of the class would lead another to mutually shared realizations. With this group I never had to refrain from punctuating our dialogue with premature conclusions. Our timing was good; often all one hundred-plus individuals seemed to arrive at the same point together. And if a few of us ever got there first, we did not settle back and revel in our satisfaction; we kept moving with the group and shared in the exultation of the final coming together. That was a rare class, a rare experience conducted under unusually propitious circumstances, but many others have approached it in the quality of their special moments. I know, experientially, that this ideal can be real.

The Closing Testimony

It has been real, for myself and others. I would like to close with the words of two of those others, whose testimonies bear witness so well to the joy of teaching and to the exacting price one often must pay in trying to achieve that ecstatic or erotic educational experience in an institutional context. Terrence Todd, another contributor to *The New Teachers* (1972), describes his feeling after witnessing a moving dialogue among students in his class: "During this whole electric exchange, I sat still, saying nothing, but if the thought that I didn't get my pedagogical rocks off on this scene is present, a rereading of the title ["Coming Together"] would be in order" (p. 142). Todd continues, "I no longer am satisfied to stand apart from my students and jockey with them for position, playing oneupmanship in the deadly game of grades." He concludes: "As a teacher, then, and as a man, my *raison d'etre* is to come together with my students and be of good service" (p. 148). With a few more open and honest voices such as Todd's, we will be much closer to Fiedler's desired vocabulary for understanding and appreciating the potentially erotic nature of teaching.

Perhaps the most important voice to date is that of Sylvia Ashton-Warner in her incomparably authentic memoir, *Teacher* (1963). It is a long way from my own situation in a representative state multiversity in New Mexico to Ashton-Warner's one-room schoolhouse full of Maori five-year-olds in New Zealand. Though I may not agree with all of her attitudes toward the children with whom she worked and played, I had to cheer (literally—breaking the predawn silence) when I first read these words: "When I teach people I marry them. . . . They had to be part of me. . . . They become part of me, like a lover. The approach, little different. The askance observation first, the acceptance next, then the gradual or quick coming, until in the complete procuration, there glows the harmony, the peace. . . . All the rules of love-making apply to these spiritual and intellectual fusions. . . . I'm glad I know this at last, that to teach I need first to espouse" (p. 211-212).

One hesitates to delineate what Ashton-Warner calls the rules of love-making. I hope we have helped reveal the potentially analogous natures of love-making and teaching-learning. I suggest that the vocabulary which Fiedler sought would include sharing, touching, authenticity, transparency, compassion, communication, silence, joy, ecstasy, pain, arousal, awakening, trust, desire, doubt, recognition, blinding and binding, fearing and freeing—and, of course, opening up and coming together.

The mind must feel, the body think, in order for the self to be. Our academic tradition—which would divorce reason and emotion, intellect and intuition, content and consciousness, knowledge and the knower— produces stasis and stagnation in the name of stability. The knowing and knowledge which characterize loving and learning at their best must be both verbal and visceral. As student, to know a learned person must be to know the person learning. To share what we know, we teachers must give of ourselves so that knower and known may grow. If I am to learn or to love, I must be at one with my self and the other; in that moment of at-one-ness, the moment of atonement, I can share the poignancy of learning and loving—the meaning of living.

References

Altman, I. and Taylor, D. *Social Penetration: The Development of Interpersonal Relationships.* New York: Holt, Rinehart and Winston, 1973.

Ashton-Warner, S. *Teacher.* New York: Simon and Schuster, 1963.

Axelrod, J. *The University Teacher as Artist.* San Francisco: Jossey-Bass, 1973.

Eble, K. E. *A Perfect Education.* San Francisco: Jossey-Bass, 1966.

Eble, K. E. *The Aims of College Teaching.* San Francisco: Jossey-Bass, 1983.

Elbow, P. "Freedom and Constraint in Teaching." In D. M. Flournoy (Ed.), *The New Teachers.* San Francisco: Jossey-Bass, 1972.

Emerson, R. W. "The American Scholar." In C. D. Mead (Ed.), *"The American Scholar" Today: Emerson's Essay and Some Critical Views.* New York: Dodd, Mead, 1970.

Epstein, J. *Masters: Portraits of Great Teachers.* New York: Basic Books, 1981.

Ericksen, S. C. *The Essence of Good Teaching.* San Francisco: Jossey-Bass, 1984.

Fiedler, L. A. "Book Review of *The Politics of Literature: Dissenting Essays on the Teaching of English.*" *Change,* 1972, *4,* 63–66.

Flournoy, D. M. (Ed.). *The New Teachers.* San Francisco: Jossey-Bass, 1972.

Freire, P. *Pedagogy of the Oppressed.* New York: Herder and Herder, 1970.

Greene, M. *Landscapes of Learning.* New York: Teachers College Press, 1978.

Jourard, S. M. *The Transparent Self.* New York: Van Nostrand Reinhold, 1964.

Kline, M. *Why the Professor Can't Teach: Mathematics and the Dilemma of University Education.* New York: St. Martin's Press, 1977.

Leonard, G. *Education and Ecstasy.* New York: Delacorte Press, 1968.

Lowman, J. *Mastering the Techniques of Teaching.* San Francisco: Jossey-Bass, 1984.

Macrorie, K. *A Vulnerable Teacher.* Rochelle Park, N.J.: Hayden Book Company, 1974.

Macrorie, K. *Twenty Teachers.* New York: Oxford University Press, 1984.

Morris, W. H. *Effective College Teaching.* Washington, D.C.: American Council on Education, 1970.

Paternite, C. E. "Teaching Philosophies and Methods: A Developmental Perspective." In P. A. Lacey (Ed.), *Revitalizing Teaching Through Faculty Development.* New Directions for Teaching and Learning, no. 15. San Francisco: Jossey-Bass, 1983.

Taylor, H. *Students Without Teachers.* New York: McGraw-Hill, 1969.

Todd, T. "Coming Together." in D. M. Flournoy (Ed.), *The New Teachers.* San Francisco: Jossey-Bass, 1972.

Joel M. Jones is vice president for Administration and Planning at the University of New Mexico. As professor of American Studies he teaches one course each semester, thereby keeping touch with the raison d'etre for administration and developing the experiential base for his writings on education, social history, and literature.

The editor provides further suggestions and resources for developing communication skills.

Meeting the Challenge

Jean M. Civikly

For reasons discussed in the first chapter of this volume, faculty often express embarrassment about seeking help in improving their teaching. Fortunately, there are many ways of working on one's instructional communication skills without even drawing attention to oneself. The suggestions made in this chapter are designed for such individual development. They include three challenges: (1) familiarize oneself with the literature on recommended teaching communication behaviors; (2) make use of the resources within oneself and those available through the institution; and (3) practice.

Familiarize self with literature. The academic disciplines of educational research, educational psychology, speech communication, theater, and higher education are central reading reservoirs for communication behaviors pertinent to classroom instruction. Is it possible that these disciplines could agree on recommendations for instructional communication skills? The answer is yes. Table 1 contains several examples, with varying degrees of specificity, that should illustrate the communication skills frequently discussed as the nuts and bolts of effective teaching.

If the most important of these behaviors were to be singled out, two would emerge: clarity and enthusiasm. In his recent work, *Enhancing Adult Motivation to Learn* (1985), Raymond Wlodkowski provides several checklists for assessing levels of enthusiasm and clarity. These lists are strongly recommended both for student feedback and self-assessment.

J. M. Civikly, (Ed.). *Communicating in College Classrooms.*
New Directions for Teaching and Learning, no. 26. San Francisco: Jossey-Bass, June 1986.

Table 1. A Sampler of
Recommended Instructional Communication Behaviors

Murray's Teacher Behaviors Inventory (1985)

Enthusiasm

Speaks expressively or emphatically
Moves about while lecturing
Gestures with hands and arms
Shows facial expressions
Uses humor
Reads lecture verbatim from notes (negatively correlated)

Clarity

Gives multiple examples
Stresses important points

Interaction

Addresses students by name
Encourages questions and comments
Praises students for good ideas
Asks questions of class

Rapport

Friendly, easy to talk to
Shows concern for student progress

Organization

Signals transition to new topic

Wlodkowski's Cornerstones of a Motivating Instructor (1985)

Expertise

Knows something beneficial to adults
Knows the subject well
Is prepared to convey knowledge through instruction

Empathy

Has realistic understanding of students' needs and expectations
Adapts instruction to students' level of expertise and skill
Continuously considers the students' perspectives

Enthusiasm

Cares about and values what is taught, both for self and students
Expresses commitment to learning with appropriate degrees of emotion, animation, and energy

Clarity

Provides students with alternative instruction if initial presentation is unclear
Instruction is understood and followed by most students

Lowman's Model of Effective College Teaching (1984)

Intellectual Excitement

Low: vague and dull
Moderate: reasonably clear and interesting
High: extremely clear and interesting

Interpersonal Rapport

Low: cold, distant, highly controlling, unpredictable
Moderate: relatively warm, approachable, democratic, and predictable
High: warm, open, predictable, highly student-centered

Table 1. A Sampler *(continued)*

Perry's Instructor Expressiveness Construct (1985)

Physical Movement
Voice Inflection
Eye Contact
Humor

Make use of resources of self and institution. The second challenge for working on one's communication skills is to make use of the resources within oneself and those available through the institution. What resources might an individual already possess? We all have bodies, faces, and voices— the basic tools for communicating the knowledge in our minds. These communication tools must not be discounted as inconsequential to learning. In her chapter on nonverbal communication by instructors, for example, Janis Andersen addresses how these nonverbal dimensions affect instruction.

In addition to basic skills, we all have other internal resources, including our attitudes about teaching and about students and our interest in the course content and level of instruction. Our personal resources also include the characteristics cited by Eble (1972) as promoting or discouraging effective teaching. The promoting characteristics include generosity, discipline, energy, variety, examples, honesty, and a sense of balance and proportion. The discouraging characteristics are Eble's seven deadly sins of teaching: arrogance, dullness, rigidity, insensitivity, vanity, self-indulgence, and hypocrisy. Each of these characteristics comes across to students through the teacher's manner and style of communicating. Depending on how the teacher chooses to communicate with the class, he or she *can* influence and direct what image and relationship is developed with the students. Just as cynicism can breed cynicism, so can enthusiasm breed enthusiasm.

As for resources available through the teaching institution, there are many. Some of these are organized programs, formal instructional sessions, and teaching consultations. Others have a more anonymous and unassuming nature and can be used more informally. The first institutional resource bank is the library and its holdings pertinent to higher education and teaching effectiveness. These include such books as *A Practical Handbook for College Teachers* (Fuhrmann and Grasha, 1983), *Speech Communication for the Classroom Teacher* (Cooper, 1984), *Mastering the Techniques of Teaching* (Lowman, 1984), *Communication in the Classroom* (Barker, 1982), *The Craft of Teaching* (Eble, 1976), *Effective Group Discussion* (Brilhart, 1982), *Teaching Tips* (McKeachie, 1985), and *Teaching as Performing* (Timpson and Tobin, 1982).

Periodicals provide the most recent articles on educational research and applications relevant to effective instructional communication. Perusal of the following journals should be worthwhile: *Change* Magazine, *Col-*

lege Teaching, the *Journal of Educational Psychology, Communication Education, Theory into Practice,* the *American Educational Research Journal,* and the *Journal of Higher Education.* The library or office of faculty development may also have handbooks on instructional training developed for the university's teaching assistants and faculty. Although these materials are designed primarily for teaching assistants, they include many practical suggestions and condensed information for instructional communication. Examples of these handbooks are *Teaching at Stanford* (Fisher, 1981), *Mentor,* (Farris, 1985), *Teaching Assistant Resource Center Handbook* (Civikly, 1983), *Ready, Set, Teach!* (New Mexico State University, 1985), and *Improving Your Lecturing* (Diamond and others, 1983). Newsletters designed for faculty development are also helpful resources (see, for example, Kansas State University's *Exchange* newsletter, published by the Center for Faculty Evaluation and Development).

Other resources for monitoring one's own communication skills include tape recording equipment, both audio and video. The inconspicuous placement of a small audio cassette recorder in the classroom can provide a wealth of information for self-assessment. Such vocal qualities as tone, volume, rate, pitch, fluency (absence of uhs, ums, okays, etc.), the use of pauses, and the attitudes and emotions conveyed by them is enlightening. In his book *Mastering the Techniques of Teaching* (1984), Joseph Lowman offers several good suggestions for using audio recorders and vocal exercises to strengthen one's oral presentation. Video recording is a bit more obtrusive, but with state-of-the-art equipment it can be accomplished without extreme interruption or distraction to the class proceedings. A portable camera can be procured from the university's media center or possibly from a teacher's or student's own home system. Review of the videotape is truly worth a thousand words. In using videotapes for training teaching assistants, I have found that each assistant can identify instances of superior, moderate, and mediocre performance. Once viewed on videotape, distracting behaviors can be pinpointed and alterations can be considered. Follow-up taping is a perfect means of checking the adjustments and their effects.

Last but not least, another resource available through the institution is the experience of our colleagues. Occasional visits to each other's classes can provide new ideas for handling material and alternatives for instruction. Such visits also provide a basis and an opportunity to talk about teaching with colleagues—the problems, successes, enjoyments, and disappointments, what works, and what does not. Such conversations may become a channel for expressing concerns and interest in teaching approaches and instructional successes and, in the process, may help to break the ice for other professors to feel comfortable in joining the discussion.

Practice. This third challenge for working on one's communication skills is a must. Experiment with different techniques and behaviors. Keep what you like and what works, and refine it even more. Put aside the techniques that do not work for another time or course or group of students. Try out a variety of methods (lectures, group work and discussions, demonstrations, role plays, visual materials, and so forth). After giving each method a fair review, select methods that suit you and the students best. Using myself as an example, my upper limit of lecturing is between fifteen and twenty minutes, and my preferred style is student participation through large class and small group tasks and discussions. My own teaching satisfaction and the students' positive reactions tend to support my teaching mode.

Practice of skills can also be accomplished through formalized outlets operating in many communities: the adult continuing education programs and classes offered by colleges, public schools, and community centers. These programs are scheduled most often in the evenings or late afternoons and on Saturday mornings. Offerings may be for credit or not, and if offered through the university, faculty may have a waiver of tuition fees. Offerings pertinent to instructional communication skills might have such titles as "Group Leadership Training," "Public Speaking Enrichment," "Storytelling for Adults," "Reducing Communication Anxieties," "Interpersonal Communication Skills," and "Basics of Acting." Such courses can mend the ragged spots, provide an outlet for interacting with a wider spectrum of individuals, and benefit both professional and social interactions. In addition to the information acquired, these classes provide models for performance and give safe opportunities to explore alternative approaches and applications for instructional settings.

The Payoffs

The ultimate question is now posed: Is it worth it? Why invest sacred and scarce time and energy into one's instructional communication skills? The payoffs, both professional and personal, are reported as greater enjoyment and satisfaction with one's teaching performance, and a pride that propels one to consider ways to heighten student motivation, interest, and performance. According to some professors, nothing can beat the exhilerated "high" felt when successfully teaching a class or seminar—the animated electric exchange of ideas can be exhausting in the best of ways. This sense of satisfaction can also serve to keep one going at times when faculty morale is shaken and work malaise sets in.

The professional payoffs overlap the personal ones in regard to heightened concern and energy given to good teaching. As for the students, research indicates that students recognize and appreciate energized teaching (Perry, 1985). Student ratings of instructors show a strong positive correlation with instructor expressiveness. Thus, the ultimate payoff may well be the contribution made to students and to their continued investment in learning.

98

References

Barker, L. L. (Ed.). *Communication in the Classroom.* Englewood Cliffs, N.J.: Prentice-Hall, 1982.

Brilhart, J. K. *Effective Group Discussion* (4th ed.) Dubuque, Iowa: Wm. C. Brown, 1982.

Civikly, J. M. *Teaching Assistant Resource Center Handbook.* Department of Speech Communication, University of New Mexico, 1983.

Cooper, P. J. *Speech Communication for the Classroom Teacher.* (2nd ed.) Dubuque, Iowa: Gorsuch Scarisbrick, 1984.

Diamond, N. A., Sharp, G., and Ory, J. C. *Improving Your Lecturing.* Office of Instructional Resources, University of Illinois at Urbana-Champaign, 1983.

Eble, K. E. *Professors as Teachers.* San Francisco: Jossey-Bass, 1972.

Eble, K. E. *The Craft of Teaching.* San Francisco: Jossey-Bass, 1976.

Farris, C. *Mentor: A Handbook for New Teaching Assistants.* (2nd ed.) Center for Instructional Development and Research, University of Washington, 1985.

Fisher, M. *Teaching at Stanford: An Introductory Handbook.* Center for Teaching and Learning, Stanford University, 1981.

Fuhrmann, B. S., and Grasha, A. E. *A Practical Handbook for College Teachers.* Boston: Little, Brown, 1983.

Lowman, J. *Mastering the Techniques of Teaching.* San Francisco: Jossey-Bass, 1984.

McKeachie, W. J. *Teaching Tips: A Guidebook for the Beginning College Teacher.* (8th ed.) Lexington, Mass.: D. C. Heath, 1986.

New Mexico State University. *Ready, Set, Teach! A Handbook on Teaching for Graduate Assistants.* Graduate School, 1985.

Perry, R. P. "Instructor Expressiveness: Implications for Improving Teaching." In J. G. Donald and A. M. Sullivan (Eds.), *Using Research to Improve Teaching.* New Directions for Teaching and Learning, no. 23. San Francisco, Jossey-Bass, 1985.

Timpson, W. M., and Tobin, D. N. *Teaching as Performing.* Englewood Cliffs, N.J.: Prentice-Hall, 1982.

Wlodkowski, R. J. *Enhancing Adult Motivation to Learn.* San Francisco: Jossey-Bass, 1985.

Jean M. Civikly is associate professor of Speech Communication at the University of New Mexico. In addition to her teaching and research on interpersonal dynamics of instructional communication, she is director of the university's Teaching Assistant Resource Center.

Index

A

Affective learning: importance of non-verbal communication for, 44-45
Allen, S., 64, 69
Altman, I., 51, 55, 58, 85, 91
Ambiguity: of student-teacher relationship, 18; of appropriate classroom behavior, 18-19
American College Testing (ACT) program, 24
American Educational Research Journal, 95
Andersen, J. F., 1, 22, 24, 31, 41-49, 57, 95
Andersen, P. A., 22, 31, 43, 45, 49
Anxiety: relation of humor and, 65-66
Ashton-Warner, S., 90, 91
Attraction: relation of humor and, 64-65
Attributions: explanations as, 12
Authenticity: importance of for teaching, 86
Axelrod, J., 34, 40, 85, 91

B

Balzer, L., 43, 49
Barker, L. L., 95, 97
Bateson, G., 15, 20
Baughman, M. D., 68, 69
Beavin, J. H., 44, 49
Berscheid, E., 48, 49
Bess, J. L., 6, 9
Black students: interactions of with white students in classroom settings, 16
Bloom, B. S., 44, 49
Brandes, S., 65, 69
Branon, J. M., 72, 81
Brilhart, J. K., 95, 97
Brooks, D. M., 42, 49
Bryant, J., 61, 65, 70
Buber, M., 54, 58
Buss, A., 24, 31

C

Cantor, J. R., 66, 70
Change Magazine, 95
Civikly, J. M., 1-3, 5-9, 39, 44, 49, 61-70, 93-98
Classrooms: Black-white student interactions in, 16; cultural differences among students in, 13; culture of, 14, 17-19; ethnocentrism in, 11-20; function of humor in, 66-67, 69; power hierarchy in, 66, 69; social structure of, 66; values of, 15-16, 17. *See also* Student-teacher relationship; Teaching
Coletti, S. F., 78, 82
Collaboration: for conflict resolution, 76, 78, 79-80
College Teaching, 95
Collins, M. L., 46, 49
Communication: apprehension, 1, 21-31; characteristics of, 2; competence, 6-8; definition of, 42; humor as act of, 62-63; importance of between students and teachers, 53-54; messages, 44; nonverbal, 41-49; and relationship to culture, 15; skills crucial for effective teaching, 93-94. *See also* Student-teacher relationship; Teaching
Communication Education, 95
Condon, J. C., 2, 11-20
Conflict: ability of teachers to deal with, 57; analysis of, 73-74; collaboration to resolve, 79-80; management styles, 74-76; between students and teachers, 71-82; tactics, 78. *See also* Teaching
Confrontation. *See* Conflict
Content competence, 6, 42
Cooper, P., 3, 56, 58, 95, 98
Coser, R. L., 66, 69
Courses on teaching, 97
Cultural differences: among academic disciplines, 13; between academic institutions, 13; among students in classrooms, 13

99

Culture: academic, 13, 14; of the class-room, 14, 17–19; definition of, 12–13; and relationship to communication, 15
Culture shock, 13
Cupach, W. R., 6, 9, 55, 59
Czikszentmihalyi, M., 8, 9

D

Dallinger, J. M., 66, 69
Daly, J. A., 1, 21–31
Damico, S. B., 67, 69
Darling, A. L., 62, 65, 66, 69
DeVito, J., 1, 51–59
Diamond, N. A., 96, 98
Disciplines, academic: cultural differences among, 13
Douvan, E., 56, 58
Duck, S., 57, 58

E

Eble, K. E., 8, 9, 33, 34, 40, 56, 58, 83, 84, 91, 95, 98
Education: comparison of to theater, 5–6, 9. *See also* Learning; Teaching
Educational process model. *See* Teaching
Elbow, P., 87, 88, 91
Emerson, R. M., 77, 81
Emerson, R. W., 86–87, 91
Enjoyment: and humor in college teaching, 61–70
Epstein, J., 3, 84, 85, 91
Epstein, P., 19
Ericksen, S. C., 83, 91
Eroticism: of teaching, 83, 87–88
Ethnocentrism in education, 11–20
Evaluation: of teacher humor, 68; of teacher performance, 58

F

Faculty. *See* Teachers
Farris, C., 96, 98
Fast, J., 42
Fiedler, L. A., 83, 90, 91
Fisher, M., 96, 98
Fisher, R., 79, 81
Flournoy, D. M., 87, 91
Freire, P., 87, 91

French, J. R. P., Jr., 77, 81
Freud, S., 63, 65, 69
Frost, G. E., 3
Fuhrmann, B. S., 95, 98

G

Garrison, J. P., 43, 49
Garrison, L., 22, 31
Gearing, F., 19
Gender: differences in interest in improving teaching, 56; differences in self-disclosure, 56; of instructor as basis for student expectations, 66
Glaser, S. R., 27, 31
Goodchilds, J. D., 66, 69
Goodenough, W., 13, 20
Gould, L., 68, 70
Granrose, J. T., 8, 9
Grasha, A. E., 95, 98
Greene, M., 83, 91
Gruner, C. R., 65, 69

H

Hall, E. T., 15, 17, 20
Handbooks on teaching, 95–96
Harrison, R., 15, 20
Hidden curriculum, 19
Highet, G., 53, 58, 61–62, 69
Hocker, J. L., 1, 57, 71–82
Homan, S., 6, 9
Hopkins, R., 15, 20
Howell, R. W., 65, 69
Humor: as act of communication, 62–63; and the enjoyment of college teaching, 61–70; in group interaction and leadership, 67; relation to attraction, anxiety, and power, 64–67; research on in teaching and learning, 61, 63, 65, 67; as teaching tool, 62; theories and effects of, 63–64

I

Immediacy behavior: definition of, 45; role of in communication, 45–46
Institutions, academic: cultural differences between, 13
Interpersonal relationships. *See* Relational development

J

Jackson, D. D., 44, 49
James, M., 54, 58
Jamieson, D. W., 72, 81
Jensen, A. D., 45, 49
Joking relationship: analysis of, 65.
  See also Humor
Jones, J. M., 2, 83-91
Jourard, S. M., 55, 58, 86, 91
Journal of Educational Psychology, 95
Journal of Higher Education, 95

K

Kansas State University's *Exchange*
  Newsletter, 96
Kaplan, R. M., 65, 69
Keith, L. T., 43, 49
Kennedy, J. G., 65, 70
Kilmann, R., 75, 76, 81
Kline, M., 86, 91
Knapp, M. L., 51, 58
Kochman, T., 16, 20
Koestler, A., 63, 70
Krathwohl, D. R., 44, 49
Krug, L., 51, 58

L

Lawrence, D. H., 69, 70
Learning: importance of student-
  teacher relationship for, 53; role of
  nonverbal communication in,
  44-45. See also Teaching
Lederer, W. J., 57, 58
Leonard, G., 84, 91
Levine, J., 68, 70
Levinger, G., 51, 54, 58
Life-cycle perspective: used to com-
  pare teaching to personal relation-
  ship, 53-54
Love, act of: and teaching, 83-91
Lowman, J., 6, 9, 85, 91, 94, 95, 96, 98;
  model of effective college teaching,
  94

M

McCroskey, J. C., 22, 23, 24, 25, 31
McKeachie, W. J., 95, 98
Macrorie, K., 85, 87, 91

Management of conflict: styles for,
  74-76
Martineau, W. H., 64, 65, 70
Masia, B., 44, 49
Mehrabian, A., 43, 46, 49
Miller, G. R., 55, 58
Minority students. See Black students
Morris, W. H., 85, 91
Mulac, A., 25, 31
Murray, H. G., 6, 9, 94, 98; teacher
  behaviors inventory, 94

N

New Mexico State University, 96, 98
Nonverbal communication. See Com-
  munication
Norms, cultural, 12
Norton, R. W., 1, 33-40

O

Ory, J. C., 96, 98

P

Pascoe, G. C., 65, 69
Paternite, C. E., 86, 91
Peace Corps: and American and Third
  World values, 15-16
Perry, R. P., 94, 97, 98; instructor
  expressiveness construct, 94
Personal Report of Communication
  Apprehension (PRCA), 25
Pettigrew, L. E., 43, 49
Plomin, R., 24, 31
Power: analysis of, 77; and conflict,
  74; relation of humor and, 66-67;
  role of nonverbal communication
  in conveying, 48; struggles between
  student and teacher, 76-78
Prince, N., 66, 69
Public speaking anxiety, 29-30. See
  also Communication
Purkey, W. W., 67, 69
Putnam-Wilson Conflict Behavior
  Scale, 76, 81

R

Radcliffe-Brown, A. R., 64-65, 70
Raven, B. H., 77, 81

Relational development: bases for, 62–63; models of, 51–52; research applicable to, 58; skills important for, 55–57; teaching as, 51–58

Relationships. *See* Relational development

Research: applicable to relational development, 58; on connection of humor to attraction, anxiety, and power, 64–67; on humor in group interaction and leadership, 67; on humor in teaching and learning, 61, 63, 65, 67; on theories and effects of humor, 63–64

Richmond, V. P., 25, 31

Rogers, M. A., 78, 82

Rosenfeld, L. B., 44, 49, 56, 58, 62, 70

Rubin, R. B., 6, 9

Ruesch, J., 15, 20

S

Savary, L., 54, 58

Schuetz, J. E., 74, 81

Self-disclosure: importance of, for teaching, 86

Sharp, G., 96, 98

Sillars, A. L., 78, 82

Skinner, B. F., 56, 58

Smith, H. A., 42, 49

Snow, C. P., 13, 20

Social structure of classroom: and humor, 66, 69; and power, 66–67

Spitzberg, B. H., 6, 9, 55, 59

Stage fright. *See* Public speaking anxiety

Status: role of nonverbal communication in conveying, 48

Steinberg, M., 55, 58

Students: cultural differences among, 13; effect of humor on comprehension and retention of, 65; interactions among black and white, 16. *See also* Student-teacher relationship

Student-teacher relationship: ambiguity in, 18; conflict in, 57, 71–82; educational process model proposed for, 54–55; humor in, 62–70; importance of, 51, 53–54; importance of gender of instructor for, 66; power struggles in, 76–78; relational bases of, 62–63, 66; skills important for teacher in, 55–57

Styles: of conflict management, 74–76; in teaching, 33–40

T

Tactics: in managing conflicts, 78

Tamborini, R., 67, 70

Taylor, D., 51, 55, 58, 85, 91

Taylor, H., 83, 91

Teachers: ability of to deal with conflict, 57; ambiguous relationship of with students, 18; ethnocentrism of, 14, nonverbal behavior as instructional asset of, 42

Teacher-student relationship. *See* Student-teacher relationship

Teaching: analysis of styles of, 34–39; as an act of love, 83–91; courses on, 97; dramatic style of, 37, 39; educational process model of, 54–55; eroticism of, 83, 87–88; handbooks on, 95–96; humor and enjoyment in, 61–70; humor as tool in, 62, 63–64; importance of self-disclosure for, 86; as relational development, 51–58; relational skills important for, 55–57; research on role of humor in, 61; suggestions for improving skills of, 93–98

Teaching-learning process. *See* Learning; Teaching

Theater: and education, 5–6, 9

Theory into Practice, 95

Third World values: and American values, 15–16

Thomas, K. W., 72, 75, 76, 81

Thomlison, T. D., 54, 58

Timpson, W. M., 6, 9, 95, 98

Tobin, D. N., 6, 9, 95, 98

Todd, T., 90, 91

Tornatzky, L. G., 43, 49

U

Ury, W., 79, 81

V

Values: of American university compared to Third World values, 15–16; of mainstream U.S. culture in classrooms, 17

Van Kleeck, A., 24, 31
Van Riper, C., 85, 91

W

Walster, E. H., 48, 49
Wandersee, J. H., 68, 70
Watzlawick, P., 44, 49
Wheeless, L. R., 22, 31
White students: interactions of with
  black students in classroom settings,
  16
Wiemann, J., 25, 31

Wiggins, J., 35, 40
Wilmot, W. W., 72, 73, 76, 77, 78, 80,
  81, 82
Wlodkowski, R. J., 93, 94, 98
Woolfolk, A. E., 42, 49
Wulff, D., 42, 49

Z

Zigler, E., 68, 70
Zillman, D., 61, 65, 66, 67, 70
Ziv, A., 63, 70